101 WAYS
TO BE YOUNG
AT ANY AGE!

Practical Wisdom to Reverse
Your Aging, STARTING NOW...

By Bob and Fran German

Dedications

We dedicate this book to ...

- All of you who chose to "live young!" You continually invoke a positive outlook, maintain a vibrant and youthful vitality and inspire those around you.

- All of you who aspire to make healthful and meaningful changes in your lives regardless of age or life circumstances.

- To our children – Robin, Leslie, and Rich and grandchildren – Jordan, Taylor, Ryan, and Joe. We've tried our best to be role models and good parents and grandparents, although admittedly not typical. We could have done better by expressing to you more of what has been in our hearts. We love you more than we can ever say.

- All of our friends, students, and strangers, too, who took the time to contact us with inspiring comments on how our writing has positively influenced their lives.

Acknowledgments

We thank and appreciate ...

- Our daughter, Robin, who was our adviser, supporter, and co-developer of our popular Young At Any Age newsletter series. She did so much to help us.

- Our many friends who encouraged us to compile our thoughts and ideas into this book.

- And a special thanks to all of you who have purchased this book.

May reading this book help you in ways both big and small and provide some guidance to Be Young At Any Age.

Health. Harmony. Happiness.

Social Responsibility

Through our many years of travel to more than 75 countries, many 3rd world, we have seen first-hand the chilling consequences of human trafficking and child exploitation primarily for the sex trade. This is modern-day slavery.

There are an estimated 36 MILLION enslaved people in the world today! Next to drug trafficking, the trafficking of people is the second biggest business on our planet! It goes on everyday...everywhere. Slaves are cheap to buy...the average cost worldwide of a slave today is just $90!

Over the years, it has become our passion to help end child trafficking. Our intention is to increase awareness of this problem and to raise funds to help prevent this by empowering impoverished communities with a focus on education and health services.

We will be donating 100% of the proceeds from sales of this book to countering this serious problem, one child at a time.

With Gratitude,
Bob and Fran German
Co-Founders of Bob and Fran's ACT Project ... to Abolish Child Trafficking
Website: www.bobnfran.com
Email: bobnfran@bobnfran.com

Important Message

It is our hope that you enjoy and benefit from the contents of this book. It has lots of information and ideas aimed at improving the health and well-being of its readers.

Please understand that we are not licensed health professionals and not engaged in providing health-oriented services in this book. It is simply a sharing of insights and tips that we have learned and practice everyday. These have enabled us and many others to enjoy a healthy and happy life.

Please get your doctor's approval before trying any new health regimen, including but not limited to diet and exercise.

In order to further cover our butts, we specifically disclaim all responsibility for any liability, loss, or risk that is incurred by the use and application of any of this book's contents.

We are happy to have you join us in living young and well at any age.

Wisdom From Our Life's Journey

Insights for a Healthy Body, Calm Mind, and Lifted Spirit

Welcome!

Our purpose for this book is for readers to discover how to add more years to their lives and more life to their years!

Whether you are 37 or 73, we want you to know that growing older does not have to mean getting sicker and that the aging process can actually be reversed. We are living proof and there are growing numbers like us.

In this book, we share our philosophy of "growing younger, healthier, and happier – beginning at any age!" It is the result of the knowledge, wisdom, research, and experience we have acquired during our personal incredible journey through life.

We have gained insights from years of worldwide travel. We have met wisdom teachers from all corners of our planet. In addition, both of us have overcome life-threatening diseases. These all directly reflect our own lifestyle choices today and have allowed us to enjoy a wonderful healthy and happy life. And as we now enter our eighth decade on this earth – we feel better and younger than ever!! You can do the same!

This book is a compilation of brief articles and essays offering a variety of hands-on ideas to enlighten as well as to inspire you to act on them. They are based on what we personally do and how we live. These short but powerful "nuggets" of wisdom will equip you to start reversing your age at once – to feel, think, look and act younger!

Using our tips and recommendations helps accomplish what noted anthropologist Ashley Montagu said: **"The idea is to die young ... as late as possible!"** That's it! That's the goal!

You can enjoy a more meaningful, healthful, and youthful way of living, starting today!

Bob & Fran German

101 WAYS
TO BE YOUNG
AT ANY AGE!

Practical Wisdom to Reverse
Your Aging, STARTING NOW...

By Bob and Fran German

Table of Contents

#1

GOOD TIMES and
NOT-SO-GOOD TIMES

Recognize that all of life is impermanent! All of us and everything around us is ever-changing. Even when you sit still, the cells in your body are changing. Understand that because of this the good times in our lives don't last. But neither do the bad times.

So, in order to keep our minds at peace, it is important to accept both the good and not-so-good things that come into our existence. We do this knowing nothing (no thing) will last and we should simply "go with the flow" of life ... rowing downstream, instead of resisting and rowing upstream. What you resist will continue to persist.

And so it is.

#2
MORNING HOUR OF POWER

An important key to being young at any age is to stay as healthy as possible. One great way to accomplish this is to implement a daily regimen we call the "Hour of Power." This would be your every-morning routine for your mind, body, and spirit. Here's a suggested itinerary for you to consider:

1. Start your morning drinking a glass of warm water to which you have added the juice of one fresh lemon. This will help make your pH alkaline. (Research indicates that cancer cells cannot survive in an alkaline environment!)

2. Do 5-10 minutes of gentle stretches and warm-up exercises (preferably in the style of qigong or yoga).

3. Next, walk briskly for at least 20 minutes. Have clothing and shoes ready to go! Try to walk in a park or somewhere near trees and plants or in your neighborhood. JUST WALK!

4. Follow your walk with 5-10 minutes of quiet sitting with a single focus on your breath. Feel the breath entering and exiting at your nostrils. Whenever your mind wanders, simply bring your attention back to your breath. Breathe easy. Don't judge or force your breath. Enjoy this quiet time to clear your mind.

5. Now's the time to shower/bathe, groom, and dress.

6. For breakfast eat a bowl of fresh seasonal fruit with a small handful of raw nuts. Please, no sugar, eggs, milk, or bread products. Just fruit and nuts.

7. Last, take a few seconds to close your eyes and declare your intention to make it a great day by

being mindful, acting kindly to everyone, and serving others in some way.

There's true power in this morning routine. It will keep you fit, energized, happy, and healthy. Make your "Hour of Power" a daily ritual. It can change your life forever!

*Please note that we recommend participating in a complete professionally taught fitness program like qigong, tai chi, yoga, pilates, or similar in addition to the morning Hour of Power. Being physically active is fun and a necessary component to Being Young At Any Age.

#3

EXPRESSING GRATITUDE

Years ago we discovered a wonderful method for starting the day on a very positive note. When we awake from our night's sleep, we lay in bed for a few minutes recounting all the things for which we are grateful.

We mentally list them ... without rushing ... giving "feeling" to each one expressed. Some can be repeated every morning. New ones can be added anytime. This is our way of "counting our blessings." It can set the tone for realizing that this new day is a true gift ... filled with people and circumstances we deeply appreciate.

#4

NEVER MIND (MAI PEN RAI)

Here's a wonderful principle that we learned during our yearly extended stays in Thailand. It's called "Mai Pen Rai." (Pronounced My Pen Rye.) It is the Thai phrase for "never mind." In the West, when we say "Never Mind!" it can be the result of a disagreement and we usually turn and walk away in a huff. But in the Thai language, it literally means to put it out of your mind ... it's not so important.

Several years ago we were standing in front of a shop in Chiang Mai in Northern Thailand waiting for a friend. A public bus stopped near us. Behind the bus was a young man on a motor scooter. He couldn't stop fast enough and his scooter slid on its side. To our horror, he and the scooter slid under the bus. Of course, the driver had no idea of what had just happened and the bus pulled away. The young man then got up, brushed himself off, righted his scooter, said "Mai Pen Rai," smiled and went on his way! This outlook is built into the culture of this 95% Buddhist country. But we know first-hand that it can work everywhere, also! ;) It's up to us.

So the idea here is that nothing (no thing) is that important for you to lose your cool, get upset, and become totally stressed out. Next time someone spills something on your new sweater, cuts you off in traffic, you accidentally delete something off your computer, or a repairman doesn't show up (you get the idea) ... just say "Mai Pen Rai" and put it out of your mind. In the end it really wasn't that important.

#5
EASY WEEKLY CLEANSE

Nutritional cleansing is a very effective way to strengthen your immune system, improve metabolism, release toxins from your body, and also lose some weight. Pick one day of the week as your cleansing day. On this day avoid bread, grains, legumes, dairy, and animal products. Be sure to drink 6-8 glasses of purified water and herbal tea during the day. For between meal snacks, have celery or carrot sticks.

A typical cleansing menu should include:

Breakfast – a fresh fruit salad and 1 oz raw nuts

Lunch – leafy fresh vegetable salad with sunflower or other seeds and oil-free dressing

Dinner – glass of fresh vegetable juice, a fresh mixed salad with oil-free dressing, and steamed vegetable platter or mixed vegetable soup or baked potato

Cleansing is a step toward better health. It will help wash out any toxins that may have built up in your body during the week.

*Please note that we strongly urge you to get your doctor's permission before trying any new lifestyle/dietary regimen.

#6

INTENTIONS FOR THE DAY

Here's a terrific idea to help you make your day a young and happy one! It will serve the same purpose for those people you interact with as well. Every morning make it your specific intention to touch the hearts of others. Here are three examples:

1. Pay a compliment to 3 people you never interacted with before. "Great shirt!" "You look especially nice today." "Thank you for doing so much good for our community." "You have the greatest smile!"

2. Invite someone to do something special with you. "Lunch?" "Morning walk in the park?" "Catch a movie?" "Joint dinner together?"

3. Do an unexpected good deed for a shut-in or a person going through a tough time. Do their shopping or drive them. Sit with them at their doctor's appointment. Bring them a bunch of flowers and chat for awhile. Phone an old friend who lives far away.

These acts of loving kindness will "make" their day and yours, too! You'll be taking the attention off yourself and your problems (always a good thing) and lifting the spirits of people around you.

Why not start this tomorrow?

#7
THE MEANING OF LIFE

We have often been asked, "What is the meaning of life?" Our answer is "The meaning of life is a life with meaning." It's all about what we give and not what we get! Helping others creates a true "win-win" situation. When we devote our time and attention to helping the poor, sick, lonely, or disadvantaged, it becomes our path to more happiness, vitality, and less stress.

How enriching and satisfying each day becomes when we take the focus off ourselves and place it on others. Acts of kindness take your mind off your own problems and serve to improve the lives of others ... young and old, near and far, people who are close by, and those who we will never meet.

There are countless ways to live a purposeful life. From cheering up family and friends to volunteering at a place that serves the needy. It could be volunteering at a food bank, a hospital, a faith community, or crisis center. It could be teaching reading to adults, delivering Meals on Wheels, tutoring children, and much more.

We are sure that many of you are involved in service to others, but we can all do more. And for those who don't, or say they don't have the time, we encourage you to get involved starting small. It will change your life in ways you cannot imagine.

Remember that the best exercise in the world is reaching down to help someone up!

#8

X-RATED LANGUAGE

This one is not what you may think it is! It's a reminder to be more tuned-in to what you say, how you phrase it, and to work to eliminate all unwholesome and unproductive speech. What comes out of our mouths can be harmful to others and in the end harmful to ourselves. Here are some suggested ways to watch your language:

- Refrain from harsh speech that includes hurtful words.

- Be careful of false speech including lies, half-lies, falsification of facts, and gross exaggerations.

- Stop all malicious speech against people and circumstances.

- Avoid gossiping about others and spreading rumors of any kind.

- Make a strong effort to rid your language of complaining, criticizing and condemning.

- Eliminate self-absorbed non-productive phrases like, "I'm too busy," "I don't have time," "You disappoint me," "I know I'm right," "You are wrong," "It's my way or no way," "It's all your fault," "I'm not as lucky as you," "I'm in a bad mood," "I'm bored," "He is always ..." or "It is never ..." and similar expressions.

- Think before you speak! Much of what is spoken is out of habit or frustration. Whatever the reason, it reflects on you in a negative way and it is unhealthy.

- Don't raise your voice in anger or frustration! Speak softly and you'll be listened to better.

- Become more aware of what you say and how you say it.

#9
BE YOUR OWN HEALTH ADVOCATE

Remember back when doctors were able to spend much more time with each patient? Yes, they even made house calls! Now, in many cases, doctors spend as little as 7 minutes per patient – barely enough time to write a prescription! So it is really important to ask questions and to do your own research.

Modern medicine does amazing things when it comes to repairing or replacing body parts, but there are many more effective, and less harmful ways of dealing with many illnesses than prescribing drugs. Most doctors know little, if anything, about nutrition and alternative medicine. So it's more important than ever to participate in your own health and wellness choices. The Internet can be an excellent source to learn about what other options are available to you. If your doctor gets upset with you when you ask a lot of questions, it may be time to get a new doctor, one who appreciates your inquisitive mind!

Some alternative medicine choices include naturopathy, chiropractic, functional, acupuncture, integrative medicine, massage therapy, homeopathy, Ayurveda treatment, Chinese medicine, acupressure, aromatherapy, reflexology, healing touch, and reiki. Take responsibility for your health!

#10
HOW TO REVERSE YOUR AGE, STARTING NOW

Doctors are now saying that people aren't living longer; they are just dying longer! This means that the average lifespan is longer, but the quality of life is not very good. More and more sickness and suffering. This is because most of us don't lead an intentionally healthy lifestyle. Not until we are diagnosed with an illness do we even think about changing what we eat, how much we exercise, how to reduce stress and improve our attitude.

But growing older does not have to mean growing sicker or losing mental sharpness. So, it is imperative that we take control and pro-actively start living a healthy and vibrant lifestyle beginning now! We know from our personal experience and from friends over the years that you can grow younger, not older, in body, mind, and spirit!

If this is something that you would like, the best way to start is to set a personal "life goal" for ongoing happiness, health, and enjoyment. Then every day do what you can to accomplish this. As an example, our goal in life is to "Die young ... as late a possible!" So, daily we strive for a healthy body through proper diet and exercise, a calm, stress-free mind, living in the present, and maintaining an optimistic outlook. You can use this goal or write your own. Print out this goal and put it on your bathroom mirror or refrigerator to keep it "front of mind" every day.

Your "life goal" serves as your commitment. Your daily efforts to achieve this goal are the path to positive change and improvement in all facets of your being. This plan can be the way to re-invent yourself or provide a fresh start.

Whether you are 47 or 74, you can enjoy the BEST YEARS OF YOUR LIFE – beginning now!

#11
THE NO-DIET DIET

The Problem. It's hard to feel young if you don't feel healthy and energetic. We believe we definitely ARE what we eat! The problem is that the typical Western diet has evolved into a very unhealthy combination of processed foods full of chemicals, high fructose corn syrup (sugar), salt, and fat. As a result, the average weight in this country has increased dramatically in recent years. And the number of people suffering from cancer, diabetes, COPD, hypothyroidism, heart disease, and other chronic diseases has skyrocketed. Many people blame their poor health on their genes. Yet, research has shown that only 5-10% of all disease is genetic!

The Solution. There have been dozens of different diets on the market over the years. But they all seem to be doomed to failure. Therefore, we believe that "the best diet is no diet!" Instead, choose an "eating lifestyle" that you can adopt and follow every day – one that is based on the following simple rules:

- Eat more fresh fuits and vegetables every day (preferably organic)
- Buy whole grain products (bread, pasta, cereal, rice, flour, and baked goods)
- Reduce sugar intake (avoid buying products containing high fructose corn syrup, soft drinks, and sugary snacks and desserts)
- Go low fat (eat less or better yet, eliminate meat, fish, eggs, and dairy products)
- Avoid processed foods whenever possible
- Eat smaller portions and eat more slowly

Why not start the "No-Diet Diet" tomorrow and watch your energy increase, your weight drop, and your health improve.

#12

FIVE WAYS OF MAKING
WISE CHOICES

We are fortunate that we have so many choices in life. We all have the choice of being happy or unhappy. We have the choice to get upset or to stay calm. We can choose a positive outlook or a negative one. We can choose to be an optimist or a pessimist. We can be judgmental or accept others as they are. We can be disappointed or we can make the best of things. We can complain, overreact, lash out, or we can choose to remain peaceful.

Here are 5 Ways of Making Wise Choices that will help minimize future regrets:

1. It is important to make wise choices using discernment. See the big picture before acting.

2. Make choices that do no harm to others or to yourself.

3. Avoid making quick knee-jerk choices.

4. Make choices that make you happy, lift your spirits, and cause you and others to feel good.

5. Understand that the outcome of your choices are solely your responsibility and not to be blamed on others.

Making good choices on your life journey puts you on the fast-track to growing Younger, starting at any age.

#13
AMAZING MOROCCAN LENTIL SOUP RECIPE

Of course, healthy eating is an important factor in living a young and vital lifestyle. Here's Fran's recipe for our favorite soup - perfect for any time of the year!

⇒ 1 onion diced

⇒ 2 carrots diced

⇒ 2 tsp freshly grated ginger

⇒ 5 cloves garlic minced

⇒ 2 Tbsp curry powder

⇒ 2 tsp garam masala

⇒ 5 cups vegetable broth

⇒ 1/2 c crushed tomatoes

⇒ 1/2 c brown or green lentils

⇒ 2 Yukon Gold potatoes diced

⇒ 1/2 c whole wheat orzo

Sauté onion in a little water over medium heat until brown. Reduce heat. Add carrots, ginger, garlic, curry powder, and garam masala and sauté for 1 minute. Add vegetable broth and tomatoes, stirring until tomatoes are thoroughly blended with the broth. Stir in potatoes and lentils. Bring soup to a simmer. Cover pot, reduce heat to low and cook til potatoes are tender, about 30-40 minutes. Add orzo. Cover and cook for 5 more minutes.

This is a healthy high flavor soup that never misses! It makes for an easy meal to share with friends. Serve with a mixed green salad and a hearty whole grain bread.

Astamtae bitaeamik! – "Enjoy your meal!" in Arabic!

#14
THE TIME IS NOW!

The time is now for us average citizens to come together like never before with courage and conviction to become willing agents for social change. It matters not what political party you favor, what religion you are or your economic status.

The time is now to rid ourselves of indifference.

The time is now for all of us to use goodness and loving-kindness as our power for peace and equality for everyone.

The time is now to quit complaining and criticizing about what's happening and instead turn that energy into **action** by doing good things while others may be doing bad things.

The time is now for each of us to step up and do something … anything ... to support fellow human beings in our cities and towns who are being discriminated against, harassed, wronged, enslaved, at-risk, violated, vulnerable or victimized.

The time is now for each of us to be a safety net for all those who are scared.

The time is now to gather collectively and individually to reach out and help people who are suffering and in need of allies.

The time is now to be the light in a world that is often very dark for those who are·deemed "different" in the eyes of some.

The time is now for compassion, doing good and choosing to love in every instance.

One can act through volunteering. Please consider giving of your time to serve and support others through worthwhile non-profit organizations in your community.

#15
SLOW DOWN

While modern-day life has many advantages, it also has brought with it a frenetic, fast-paced way of living with more things to do. As a result, we tend to rush through each day and time passes before we enjoy the things around us. Slowing down applies to all of us whether we are working or retired.

But we can fix this! First, we must consciously recognize when we are going too fast. And second, we need to make a concerted effort to **control our time, rather than letting time control us**!

Here are some practical ideas to slow down:

- Start by paying attention to the little and beautiful things around you. Consciously open your senses and raise your awareness of everything from birds to flowers to the kindness of others.

- Simply do fewer things and refrain from over-scheduling activities, appointments, and tasks.

- Avoid multi-tasking. Complete one task at a time while being single-focused. Take care of the most important items first.

- Plan your time so that you arrive 15 minutes early for every appointment - doctor, hairdresser, church, etc. This way you can take a few minutes upon arrival to relax, gather your thoughts, socialize or just sit quietly and breathe.

- Eat slower. Drive slower. Breathe slower.

- Refrain from responding to emails, text messages, and phone calls as they arrive. Instead, designate certain times of the day to handle this.

- Disconnect! Make a strong effort to limit your time connected to electronic devices like phones, computers, and television. From time to time, try to stay disconnected for an entire day!

- Slow down with a good book, a nature walk or introspective time alone.

- Spend quality time with family and friends. Listen to them intently with nothing around to disturb the flow.

- Be here and now! Focus totally on what you are doing in this moment. If you catch your mind wandering, just gently re-focus on what's going on now.

- Increase your awareness of when you are speeding through the day. Then take your foot off the accelerator! Make it your intention to pace yourself in a lower gear.

You will fully enjoy the experience of your slower pace and how it seems to"stretch out" your day to make it more meaningful.

Keep this slow down idea "front-of-mind" and use the above tips. Then slowly (no pun intended), but surely, you will change to an unhurried lifestyle and truly savor the 86,400 precious seconds you have in each day!

#16
BECOME MORE ALKALINE

A very important step toward overall good health is achieving the proper acid-alkaline balance, as this can affect many key functions of the body. Because the average Western diet makes us very acidic, it is critical to help your body to be more alkaline.

An inexpensive test kit can be purchased from drugstores to monitor your pH level. The balance between acid and alkaline should be at slightly alkaline. Be sure to check with your physician about this as it pertains to you.

Medical research has shown that cancer cells, parasites, yeast, and other toxins cannot survive well in an alkaline environment.

It's easy to incorporate alkaline foods in your daily routine. For example, we **drink a glass of warm water each morning to which the juice of one lemon has been added before we eat or drink anything else.** This will nourish, hydrate and alkalinize your body. Lemons and limes are acidic but actually become alkaline when consumed.

Other alkaline foods include leafy greens, root vegetables, broccoli, cabbage, and garlic. Among acid-forming foods are meats, sugar, coffee, juice and processed foods.

#17
4 GIANT STEPS TO LOWER STRESS

The bad news: Stress is unhealthy and is said by experts to be the root cause of most diseases. Stress lowers your resistance and makes it easier for disease (dis-ease) to take over. Continuous states of tension, strain or anxiety can negatively impact your health and make you older faster!

The good news: You can substantially reduce your level of stress naturally without taking harmful or habit-forming medications!

Here are 4 Steps to Lowering Stress:

1. Condition yourself to live in a steady conscious state of **equanimity – being calm and balanced, especially in the midst of difficulty.** This does not happen overnight. It is a process. Set this as your intention.

2. To accomplish this, you must make a concerted effort to heighten your awareness and "**catch yourself**" when you start getting stressed. Examples would include when anger arises, when worry sets in, when your feelings are hurt, when disagreement occurs, or when you want something to be different than it is. The idea is to totally tune-in to a potential stress-response and mindfully stay in that state of equanimity.

3. Understand that you need to **accept the reality of every life experience as it is, rather than what you think it should be or how you want it to be.** This is simply seeing the truth of the moment. Acknowledge that whatever the situation, **IT IS**

WHAT IT IS! Don't resist what is happening. Just do your best to deal with it.

4. Implement a daily period of quiet sitting or meditation to calm the mind. This is a good training for strengthening equanimity and therefore lowering stress.

Lower stress levels will make an enormous difference in your temperament and in your overall well-being.

#18
TIPS FOR BETTER SLEEP

During sleep, our bodies heal and regenerate cells so it is extremely important to get adequate sleep to stay healthy and young. However, sleep problems plague a huge portion of the population, especially as we age. Millions of people take sleeping pills on a regular basis. These are habit forming and in many cases dangerous.

Healthy Options To Enhance Your Sleep:

- **Make sleep a priority.** Set your intention to get at least 8 hours of sleep a night. This should take precedence over any other activity like watching more TV, reading, working or doing household chores.

- **Develop a pre-sleep routine.** Create a calming "ritual" that you follow each night before heading to the bedroom.

    o Start in the early evening by thinking through your day, making a to-do list for tomorrow and clearing your mental desktop.

    o Other ideas for your pre-sleep regimen are drinking chamomile tea, reading, doing some gentle qigong, and taking a soothing hot bath. These can help prepare your body for a good night's sleep.

    o When first getting into bed, we particularly like the use of the **4/7/8 breathing technique** - while lying on your back breathe in through the nose to count of 4, hold breath to count of 7, exhale through the mouth to count of 8.

Repeat 3 more times. This simple routine helps to set your brain to a sleep mode.

- **Create a sleep schedule.** It is recommended that we get about 8 hours of sleep each night - preferably from about 10 pm to 6 am, even on the weekends. Studies suggest this works the best with our body's natural rhythms.

- **Reserve your bedroom for just sleep and sex.**
  - o Refrain from eating, drinking, watching TV, using a computer/tablet, or doing work in bed.
  - o Your bedroom should be cool (between 60 and 67 degrees), dark and comfortably quiet.
  - o Consider using some sleep tools like a "white noise" machine (outside the bedroom but within hearing distance), blackout curtains, a sleep mask, earplugs, socks if you have cold feet and our favorite – aromatherapy using a mister.

- **Remove Electromagnetic Fields** (EMFs) from your bedroom. These are found in all electronic devices and emit frequencies that interfere with sleep. These include clocks, computers, TV, cell phones, tablets, etc. We personally also use a Himalayan salt lamp to help purify the air and offset the EMFs.

- **Consider using supplements** that promote sleep. Check with your doctor first. Examples would include Melatonin - take 1-5 mg sublingually at bedtime. It can be purchased at health food stores. Also, tart red cherry juice – two glasses daily (contains Melatonin) may help you sleep better.

- **Avoid naps** (try substituting simple qigong exercises), cut out the caffeine (by early afternoon), and abstain from food, alcohol, and exercise within a couple hours or longer <u>before</u> going to sleep.

Put these ideas into action and enjoy more healthful sleep. Sweet dreams!

#19
SAY "YES!"

Here's a simple and wise way to live life to the fullest. Make up your mind to go through each day being open to new experiences. These can include new social opportunities, new places, new foods, new technology, new entertainment, new ideas, new anything or anyone!

As an example, if you're invited to try Indian food for the first time, refrain from a knee-jerk reaction like "No, I don't think I'll like it" or "No, it is probably too spicy" or "No, it's not for me!" And if you encounter a friendly stranger, engage that person rather than shun him/her.

Instead of responding with a quick "no," when a choice is presented...just say "yes" and try new things and meet new people.

Taking some risks and experiencing new adventures, big or small, most often will be fun and interesting.

#20
MAKE SPACE

Here's a tip to stay calm in any situation! We believe it is wise to **allow ample space between what you experience and how you respond to it**. This means eliminating an immediate "knee-jerk" response. A quick reaction can cause confrontation, arguments, regrets, and stress.

So going forward, make a concerted effort to increase your awareness when these situations arise, accept what's going on and don't respond until you've reflected on the issue. Disciplined behavior like this keeps you composed, able to think more clearly and to act in a way that is not harmful to you or to others.

#21
LIVE MINDFULLY

Being mindful is simply paying deliberate attention to the present moment. It is a conscious ongoing connection to what's happening right NOW.

Too many of us unknowingly sleepwalk through life - not giving purposeful attention to the experience of the moment at hand. It's like living on habitual auto-pilot where the mind is constantly swept into a current of rambling thoughts. The moment passes you by.

Ask yourself if your thoughts are wandering while driving so when you arrive at your destination you really cannot remember most of that experience along the way. When you walk in a park, are you fully aware of the chirping birds or seeing the beautiful flowers or are your thoughts elsewhere? When you are showering, do you truly experience the water against your skin and fully appreciate the pleasant feeling or are you thinking ahead to what you have to do later?

Understand that any of us can become more mindful and not miss out on the beauty of the present moment. Learning to live mindfully involves an ongoing conscious effort to be fully engaged in what's going on in the moment now. So, it is important that you **heighten your awareness of being present. Then catch yourself when the mind wanders away from the present into the past or the future.** Next, **gently bring your focus back** to the existing moment. You can do it!

Here are some benefits of living mindfully:

- Enables you to be engaged and enjoy all of what life has to offer - moment to moment.

- Serves to center you, keeps you present and focused, and disables the attachment to be in the past or future.

- Fosters acceptance of the moment as it is and lessens or eliminates the desire to want things to be different.

- Frees you from automatically reverting to old habitual ways of thinking and living and opens the door to new life choices.

- Heightens your awareness, improves your listening skills, clears the mind and reduces stress.

- You can practice mindfulness daily – when washing dishes, eating your meals or doing any routine activity.

- Meditation is a training for mindful behavior. It can be as easy as sitting quietly, focusing on your breath and holding that focus. When the mind wanders, gently re-focus on the breath again. Add this practice to your day.

There is limitless enjoyment, satisfaction and inner peace that comes with this process. Why not become more and more mindful … starting today!

#22

IMPORTANCE OF VITAMIN D

Vitamin D, known as the "sunshine vitamin," helps greatly to build the immune system and has powerful health benefits according to long-term scientific studies.

Vitamin D protects brain cells. It is especially effective against neurodegenerative diseases such as Alzheimer's and Parkinson's.

Low levels of vitamin D in the blood are associated with elevated cancer risk, particularly in cancers of the breast, prostate, and colon. We recently met a doctor who works in a large hospital. He said that 5 of his associates are currently battling cancer and that all 5 have low vitamin D levels!

Vitamin D can improve the health of people with autoimmune diseases such as arthritis, lupus, diabetes and multiple sclerosis.

Although vitamin D is provided naturally by the sun, most of us don't spend enough time outdoors. Also, as we age we tend to absorb even less of it from sunlight. For these reasons, it is recommended to **consider increasing vitamin D levels through good quality supplements**.

Generally, supplementing with vitamin D3 is the best way to get your levels back to normal and to promote your body's maintenance.

Vitamin D testing is not normally a part of the routine blood work that doctors request. But it is important to have your level tested. Ask your physician what he/she recommends as a vitamin D level to provide the most optimal health benefits for you.

Tip: Take your vitamin D3 with a healthy fat-containing food to enhance absorption.

Be sure to consult with your doctor before starting or adjusting a regimen of Vitamin D3 supplementation.

#23
REMOVE TOXINS ASAP

Some of our homes are filled with countless harmful poisonous chemicals - in our **cleaning supplies, our grooming aids, even our toothpaste, and deodorant!**

Try the following ideas to reduce or do away with these toxins:

- Instead of buying expensive and possibly harmful household cleaners, use water with a little vinegar added for cleaning windows, furniture, etc.

- Many brand-name toothpastes contain carrageenan, a carcinogen, and also plastic! You can make your own healthy toothpaste with baking soda and coconut oil to which you've added a couple drops of clove or cinnamon essential oil.

- Years ago scientists determined that aluminum may be a cause of Alzheimer's Disease and may be a factor in breast cancer. Antiperspirants contain aluminum. So it is a good idea to use deodorants, not antiperspirants. There are several natural brands on the market that can be purchased at health food stores and co-ops.

Fortunately, there are many excellent NATURAL shampoos, conditioners, and hair color products available these days. Some are even being carried by many of the large supermarkets as well as health food stores and online. They are not only better for you but better for the environment as well. Shop wisely to reduce the number of toxins to which you are exposed.

#24
KEEP THE WHITE OUT OF SIGHT!

Our society seems to equate aging with illness. But they don't automatically go hand in hand. It is possible, and definitely preferable, to stay healthy - or even become more healthy - as we age by eating right!

Based on our extensive research and personal experience, one simple method to greatly enhance your health is to eliminate "white" from your diet.

Here are six ways to do it:

1. **Ditch the Sugar!** When we were growing up, the average American consumed 20 pounds of sugar a year. A recent study shows that presently Americans average 160 pounds of sugar annually! Not only does that contribute to the tremendous increase in obesity in this country, but also to the increase in cancer.

   Cancer cells LOVE sugar. In fact, glucose is used in PET scans to help find cancer! Yet oncologists give patients sweets to eat after chemotherapy treatments!! Say "no" to popular sugar substitutes like Splenda, Equal and Sweet 'N Low! They have been also proven to cause cancer. Even agave, which was thought to be healthy, contains high fructose properties. Our choices for healthy substitutes for your sweet tooth are stevia, xylitol, and maple syrup.

2. **Lose the White Flour!** Unless you have celiac disease and can't eat any wheat, you can easily substitute whole wheat flour for white. The same holds true for whole wheat pasta and pizza

crust. The whole grains offer added nutrients and fiber which helps to prevent constipation. Whenever possible, make your own bread or purchase whole grain bakery bread rather than packaged products.

3. **Forget the White Table Salt!** Instead, use Himalayan Sea Salt which contains healthy nutrients.

4. **Pass on White Rice!** Although white rice is preferable to white flour, an even better option is brown rice which contains the bran layer and provides more fiber and a delicious nutty flavor. Some Asian markets even carry red, black, or purple rice. They not only look good but taste great!

5. **Reduce or Eliminate Dairy Foods.** We all grew up with the idea that milk and milk products are good for us. The dairy industry spends a fortune promoting this concept. Unfortunately, the opposite is true. There now seems to be strong evidence that dairy products cause prostate cancer and breast cancer.

There are now many good and tasty alternatives on the market to replace cow's milk. Make sure that the one you choose is unsweetened and doesn't contain carrageenan (a known carcinogen) There are now many non-dairy milk products to choose from – almond, soy, rice, hemp, and coconut to name a few.

6. **Avoid Eggs.** We suggest reducing or totally avoiding egg consumption. Recent studies now link eggs to diabetes and cancer. Also, there are many ways to cook and bake without eggs by using substitutes like applesauce, flax seed, aquafaba, bananas, and tofu.

So, you can see how to do away with the "white" from your diet by making some healthful changes at home and when dining out.

This can prevent illness and dramatically improve your health as you age. Why not start today?

Always check with your doctor before modifying your diet.

#25
HOLDING A GRUDGE

One key to being young at any age is eliminating as much stress in your life as possible.

When you hold a grudge against someone, it means you are clinging to a stressful incident from your past. **You are allowing someone to live rent-free in your head!**

The fix for this is to first be aware when these bitter thoughts arise. Then when you realize where the mind has taken you, gently re-focus your attention from that past occurrence to the existing moment before you.

Holding a grudge is unproductive behavior and harmful to your health. Daily meditation can be a big help in training yourself to let go of negative thoughts that a grudge creates.

#26
LOVING-KINDNESS MEDITATION

We believe we all have the extraordinary power to **spread the feeling of loving-kindness and friendliness to others** near and far. This can be accomplished through an easy meditation using simple words and heartfelt feelings.

1. Choose a daily designated time to sit comfortably in a quiet place for about 10-15 minutes. Allow your body to fully relax, your mind to become calm and your heart to open. Set your intention to first fill yourself with a state of unconditional love and then to send this feeling out to others.

2. Begin by pondering all that brings you personal joy and happiness. Consider all the people and things for which you are grateful. Let this feeling well up inside of you and permeate every cell of your being. Once this positive feeling sets in, silently and slowly recite a version of the following phrase: *"I am filled with good health, happiness and loving-kindness to all."* Repeat 3 or more times.

3. Next, take this idea forward to your spouse, partner, best friend, children, and grandchildren by silently repeating the phrase: *"May you be filled with good health, happiness, and loving-kindness to all."* Picture them in your mind. Repeat inwardly 3 times.

4. Now spread this loving feeling onto others in your family and all your friends. Continue this cycle onto everyone in your community, then everyone in your state, your country and to everyone on the entire planet: *"May you be filled with good health, happiness, and loving-kindness to all."* Repeat 3 or more times.

5. Silently recite these wishes for others with heightened sensitivity. Adjust the wording in any way at any time that suits you. You can offer words for one's safety, harmony, inner peace and so on. Create the words that work for you. Breathe naturally and with ease during this meditation. Make this part of every day.

Continuing to plant these seeds of love and kindness will favorably affect you and the people to whom you are directing your good thoughts.

Always lead with your heart.

#27

HOW TO REDUCE ANGER and WORRY

Anger and worry are immobilizing emotions. They harm your health and can make you older faster. They are a result of your not being in the present moment. Anger is the consequence of clinging to something that happened in the past. Worry arises when you are thinking ahead into the future.

You can reduce or eliminate angry and worrisome thoughts by:

One – Intensifying your awareness and "**catching yourself**" when they come wandering into the mind.

Two – Intentionally and immediately **change the mind** to be in the present moment, here and now.

Three – This conscious be-in-the-moment response will strengthen with **practice**.

Understand that **you cannot think of more than one thing at a time**. So, your episodes of anger and worry will decrease by the simple act of changing your thoughts to what's happening now. Try it. It works!

#28

TAKE GOOD QUALITY SUPPLEMENTS

Farmers used to rotate their crops which allowed the soil to be more nutrient-rich.

But today it is common for the same crops to be planted every year, a practice that depletes the soil. As a result, we are not getting an adequate supply of vitamins and minerals from the produce we eat.

This makes it necessary to **supplement your diet for maximum health and vitality**. You should **discuss with your healthcare provider what supplements you should take and do some research on your own.**

We personally take a number of excellent-quality vitamins and minerals. They include vitamin C, vitamin D3, flaxseed, turmeric, CoQ10, vitamin B12, vitamin K2, plus a multivitamin. These have kept us healthy, energized and young

Unfortunately, not all supplements are created equal. Recent reports indicate that some of the brands sold in discount stores, drugstores and supermarkets are of poor quality.

It is recommended that you check with a nutritionist or someone knowledgeable about supplements in a health food store for advice.

#29

MAKE EVERY BREATH COUNT

A wise Tibetan doctor once told us that each human being is allotted a certain number of breaths in a lifetime! He said to not take breathing for granted and to slow our breathing down.

We believe in what the doctor said and think that the fewer breaths we take, the better the chance of living longer and healthier.

So, it is essential that we **intentionally practice slowing our breathing process a few times each day.** It only takes a couple of minutes and will prove to be a relaxing and enjoyable experience.

This can be accomplished by practicing simple Qigong diaphragmatic "4, 4, 4+ count" breathing.

Start by placing your hand on your belly. With your mouth closed, gently breathe in through your nose into your belly for a count of 4 so that you feel your belly expand and your hand moves forward. Now, hold the breath for a count of 4. Then finally, exhale for a count of 4 or more, also through your nose, so that your stomach moves back toward your spine. Repeat this cycle 3-6 times. If you cannot hold to a 4-count, just do what you can. Try to extend the count as you practice.

This technique can be done standing, sitting or reclining. Do your best and do it 2-3 times each day. Also, try this technique while lying in bed at night, as it can help promote better sleep.

This soothing method of breathing can also release emotional tension on the exhalation, massage your internal organs, and train your breath to slow down so you take fewer breaths per minute.

This would make the Tibetan doctor happy and help reverse your aging!

#30
STUFF HAPPENS!

It's very clear that the **lower your anxiety level, the higher your happiness quotient**. This is largely contingent on simply accepting the constant flow of experiences that come into our lives, whether they are pleasant or unpleasant. Simple ... but not easy.

So, for example, your neighbor's new dog poops on your lawn ... again! This infuriates you and leads to an argument with your neighbor. Naturally, this creates a good deal of tension. BUT, what if you refrained from over-reacting and just acknowledged the fact that literally "stuff happens!" And instead of getting mad, you met with your neighbor to discuss practical and peaceful ways of resolving this issue. No sweat. No stress.

Did we mention this was not easy? That's the bad news. But the good news is to accomplish this idea of "complete Acceptance of all circumstances" is very possible.

Here's the process to condition yourself to make this happen:

> **One** – Train yourself to recognize that, in every instance, what is happening is real. It is the Truth of the moment. These are life's realities and you cannot rewind time and change what has occurred.
>
> **Two** – Commit to yourself to purposefully Accept and not resist what's going on. Know that what you resist will continue to persist! And probably will go downhill from there.
>
> **Three** – Use discernment, common sense, and your own innate wisdom to handle and, if needed, resolve

each circumstance in a way that avoids stress and anxiety.

You hold the power of Acceptance. Use this power everyday ... and every day will be much less stressful and much happier!

#31

BEST DESSERT EVER! "NICE CREAM" RECIPE

If you love ice cream but want to eat healthy by reducing or eliminating your dairy intake, we have the perfect solution. It's our recipe for Nice Cream ... dairy-free, chemical-free, as well as no/low fat and no/low sugar depending on what you add!

It's so easy to make and very delicious. All you need are 4 ripe bananas and a food processor!

Peel bananas, cut into chunks and freeze overnight. Place frozen bananas in food processor and process until bananas are creamy. Scoop into dishes and eat or scoop individual portions into a container, cover and freeze for later. Makes 6 servings

Variations:

Add a tablespoon of chunky peanut butter, frozen strawberries or frozen blueberries before processing. Or, for chocolate Nice Cream, add a couple of teaspoons of cocoa powder.

Add dark chocolate chips and chopped walnuts to the creamed bananas before scooping.

Living young means eating smart.

Enjoy!

#32
OUR SECRET WEAPON!

This is maybe the single most important health tip we will ever share with you! It is the practice of Qigong – an ancient Chinese system of health care and well-being.

Qigong (pronounced "chee-gung") is commonly translated as "energy exercise." Those who play Qigong regularly find that it helps to prevent disease, speed up recovery from illness, increase energy, lower stress, promote healing, build stamina, and retain a youthful vitality.

Practicing Qigong has been found to strengthen the immune system, reduce blood pressure, improve balance, enable more flexibility, and enhance cardiovascular, respiratory, circulatory, lymphatic and digestive functions.

Qigong is fun and easy-to-do! A qualified instructor will lead you through a series of slow, gentle, flowing movements so you are able to cultivate and circulate healthful Qi throughout your body. You will also learn about the power of mind intent, correct body alignment, breathing techniques, plus how to calm the mind and relax the body.

Unlike most conventional exercise programs, Qigong connects the body, mind, and spirit. It encourages a positive outlook on life and helps eliminate harmful attitudes and behaviors. It also creates a balanced lifestyle that brings greater harmony, stability, and contentment. Anyone can benefit from practicing it regardless of age or ability.

On a personal level, our daily Qigong practice has forever changed our lives! It has been our "secret weapon" to help enable both of us to overcome life-threatening illnesses, protect us from getting sick, provide ongoing high energy and has actually reversed our aging. Thanks to Qigong we feel better than ever at age 77!

So, our advise to you is to seek out a qualified Qigong teacher in your area. Because of its rising popularity, you can find a teacher almost everywhere. Start by searching the internet. Find an instructor who you like.

Practice every day. It's a wonderful activity to do with your spouse, partner or a friend. We encourage you to not put this off. Act now and start enjoying the many health benefits that Qigong has to offer.

As with any exercise program, consult with your doctor before starting Qigong.

#33

HOW TO ATTRACT ANYTHING INTO YOUR LIFE

Here's one of our secrets to living a great life at any age. It's The Law of Attraction – one of the most powerful natural laws of the Universe. We personally have used it over and over again for over 50 years! It is not "foo-foo" stuff – it works! It is a guiding force for us.

Using the Law of Attraction, we are able to manifest whatever we would like into our lives ... health, happiness, friendships, abundance ... and it can work for you!

Its basic principle is as follows: **You attract into your life that which you give your energy, focus, and attention ... whether you want it or not. Good or bad, whatever you talk about, think about, and especially, feel about...will come about.** Like gravity, it is absolute, constant and unwavering. It works whether you know about it or not.

Main Points to Understand the Law of Attraction:

- View yourself as a powerful magnet that can attract anything.

- Everything we think, say and feel has an energetic vibration that reverberates to the Universe.

- The Attraction process starts with a thought ... the thought turns into an emotion (a mood or feeling) ...an emotion turns into energy (positive or negative) ... the energy turns into a vibration that resonates to the Universe. The Law of Attraction responds in like kind to whatever vibrations you send (positive or negative)...it doesn't distinguish between good or bad, positive or negative.

- You get more of whatever you vibrate. You resonate good vibes by being joyful, helpful, loving, grateful, kind, giving, and peaceful. You give off bad vibes when you are stressed, fearful, worried, selfish, doubtful, upset, and forceful.

- Positive attracts positive, negative attracts negative. Think good thoughts, attract good things. Think bad thoughts...attract bad things.

- Simply...**Like Attracts Like!**

- Understand that The Law of Attraction is continually in effect.

- You can also use this Law to intentionally manifest something particular into your life.

Five A's to Manifesting What You Want Using The Law of Attraction:

1. First, **ASK the Universe for something you wish to attract.** Do this only when you are feeling good and in an optimistic confident mood.

2. Next, **put your ATTENTION on what you would like to draw into your existence.** Ask for whatever you envision with a locked-in focused concentration and great passion. Radiate positive vibrations through visualization – seeing what you want actually happening. **Do this without clinging to an outcome and then let it go and let the Universe take over.**

3. Now, **take appropriate ACTION.** You cannot spell "attraction" without "action!" Once you know what you would like to attract, you need to **create action-steps** to help make this happen. Your actions open the door to "receive what you perceive." So, make a plan to attract what you want and ACT on it!

4. Be sure to **ALLOW what you manifest.** "Be Open and Believe so that you will receive!" Your feelings of worthiness, positive energy, and self-assurance must be vibrating in line with what you would like to attract!

5. Continually express your **APPRECIATION** for all that flows into your life by helping others – "passing it forward." Performing ongoing acts of loving kindness and making a difference in the lives of others is THE way to **show gratitude and thankfulness to the Universe.**

We all have the power to allow The Law of Attraction to work for us. Gratefully use it to enjoy amazing experiences of a vital youthful-feeling life of peace, prosperity, and purpose. We encourage you to accept your power and start using it now!

#34

THE SECRET TO READING PRODUCE LABELS

You probably have noticed that almost all produce in the supermarket has small stickers with 4 or 5 numbers on them.

Here's a short guide to what they mean:

- Four numbers indicate that the item was grown conventionally.
- If there are 5 numbers and the first one is 8, that means it is genetically modified (GMO).
- If the first of 5 numbers is 9, that item is organic.

This guide will help you to know what you are buying. We personally choose to avoid GMOs and encourage you to do your own research on this subject.

#35
BE THE OBSERVER

There is drama being played out around us all the time. Every day we can come upon conversations, discussions, debates, confrontations, and arguments. Sometimes they can be very heated. It's simply part of life.

These can arise from a variety of topics such as politics, religion, news, laws, gossip and even the actions of other people. Yet you have the choice of becoming part of the cast of players or a member of the audience.

Becoming a participant too often results in frustration and aggravation ... and your blood pressure can quickly shoot up. As an alternative, **we think it wise to consider simply being the "observer" of the drama instead of jumping into it**. It's sort of like watching a movie instead of being in it. If asked to get involved, graciously decline and just 'stay out of the fray!'

This choice is much healthier and it can be more satisfying to merely watch and listen to the story unfold. It can also be your way of making your point through non-participation. Very calm. Very cool.

Try being the "observer" more and more. It can be a positive step forward to a pattern of making stress-free choices and an overall calmer demeanor.

#36
LETTING GO...

A long time ago, a friend and Buddhist wisdom teacher taught us that holding onto thoughts that caused stress was like carrying around a heavy stone wherever you go. And that the way to relieve this mental suffering was to just let go of the heavy stone.

"Holding on" is a result of the mind clinging to an experience from the past. This clinging or attachment is the cause that negatively impacts our inner peace and affects how we act in the present. We tend to replay these memories over and over in our heads and allow regret, guilt, shame, frustration, worry, and anger to arise which become barriers to our happiness and to our health.

The good news is that there are ways to help you let go. We'll share them here:

1. **Accept the truth of past experiences and look for the positive life lessons that you learned.** Take full responsibility for your past actions and mistakes. Don't play the blame game. Ponder the wonderful possibilities to moving forward with your life.

2. **Try to bring closure to past bitter situations or relationships to which you are still attached.** This can be done through communicating your feelings to those involved, offering forgiveness, burying the hatchet, releasing a grudge and moving on – whether or not others are willing to do the same. If doing this is not possible, it can be helpful to write a letter clarifying your feelings and intentions. Even if it is never sent, it can help you come to terms with the truth of the past experience.

3. **Understand that you have options when clinging thoughts from your past arise.** You can choose to dwell on them or you can choose to move on. You also have the power to change your destructive thoughts to constructive thoughts ... unpleasant to pleasant. Refrain from wasting time and energy on things that you cannot change. Instead, focus only on what can be changed and embrace change. Remember that clinging thoughts do more harm to you than to others.

4. **Take control of your own happiness.** Do things that make you feel good and do no harm to you or others. Cultivate new friendships, new activities, take some risks and step into new life adventures. It also helps to take the attention off yourself and act to serve others through volunteering and continually performing acts of kindness, big or small, to others.

Letting go takes a decisive intentional effort. **Start by making a strong commitment to not let negative experiences from your past shape your future.** Then determine what positive steps need to be taken and act on them. Use the ideas above to get you to stop holding that heavy stone and start enjoying life to the fullest, beginning at any age.

#37

A LESSON IN PADDLING

How are you rowing your boat? Are you going with the effortless downstream flow of life or are you constantly paddling upstream against the current when life seems so difficult with lots of frustration, disappointment, and stress? Maybe it's a mix of both.

Naturally, we all want to stay in that fun, easy downstream flow where life is good. It's a matter of aligning your energy (Qi or Chi) with the Universe, God, Love or whatever your Source may be. So, we have some ideas and reminders to share that will help get your boat going in the right direction:

- Make choices and do things that make you happy, lift your spirits, and cause you to always feel good about yourself and your life.

- Be the light to others by reaching out and helping those who are feeling scared, helpless and in need of support and love.

- Continually look for things for which you are grateful, appreciate them, and give thanks for bringing them into your life.

- In all situations, accept what is happening with calmness and steadfastness while avoiding knee-jerk reactions.

- Deal with adversity and challenges in a constructive manner by eliminating self-pity and wallowing in destructive thoughts.

- Do away with the attitude of wanting things to be a specific way or expecting certain outcomes.

- Avoid any behavior that may be harmful to yourself or to anyone else.

Paddling downstream is exhilarating! It makes life fun and meaningful and fosters a youthful-feeling every day, no matter your age, health or station in life.

#38

TURMERIC – One of Our Personal Health Secrets

In our opinion Turmeric (which contains curcumin) may be one of the most effective nutritional substances in existence! It's part of our daily regimen and we believe it has served as a key supplement for staying healthy. Based on a number of high-quality studies, Turmeric is said to have the following advantages:

10 Health Benefits of Turmeric:

1. Curcumin is a natural **anti-inflammatory** which helps the body fight foreign invaders and repair damage. It has been found to be as effective as anti-inflammatory drugs without the side effects!

2. Contains powerful **medicinal properties** especially when taken with black pepper to aid absorption. (We like Gaia Turmeric Supreme with black pepper.)

3. Has powerful **antioxidant effects** and protects the body from damaging free radicals.

4. Boosts **brain** function and lowers risk of degenerative brain diseases.

5. May lower risk of **heart** disease.

6. Can help prevent, and actually treat **cancer.**

7. May possibly be useful in preventing and treating **Alzheimer's** disease.

8. Can help treat symptoms of **arthritis** sometimes more effectively than anti-inflammatory drugs.

9. Is effective in alleviating symptoms of **depression.**

10. May help **delay aging** and fight age-related chronic diseases by reducing oxidation and inflammation.

We've been using turmeric for some time. You may want to consider using it also. Check with your doctor and get his approval first.

#39

THE ART OF PEELING POTATOES

Peeling potatoes may not be a big deal to most people. But it can be a lesson in mindfulness. When you are peeling potatoes BE with the potatoes. Concentrate your full attention on the task. Be conscious of how the potato feels in your hand, watching intently as you peel, seeing the skin curl up and off. And most important, not letting the mind interrupt this single-focused attention with an array of other thoughts that take you away from the present moment of peeling and into another place in the past or future. Approach this potato peeling process as you would approach meditation. And if and when the mind does wander, be aware of this and return to the potatoes.

This should apply also when drinking your delicious hot cup of coffee in the morning. Breathe in the deep rich aroma, watch the coffee flow as you pour it into your cup, look at the steam, stop and savor the moment before the first sip, and slowly enjoy the flavor as it covers your tongue and mouth.

This is another example of being in the moment. It can apply to so much we do every day – showering, driving, cooking, eating, working, playing, relaxing.

This focused consciousness means purposefully paying attention to what's happening here and now while calmly accepting one's feelings, thoughts, and bodily sensations. It is the antithesis of "sleepwalking through much of life" like too many of us do and missing so much of it.

Being fully present with every phase of our daily regimen enriches us in mind, body, and spirit. It slows us down, heightens our enjoyment of the moment, increases our awareness and appreciation of things big and small, and seems to make each day a little longer and a lot more satisfying.

To us, this is a wonderful way to add more meaning and wisdom to each day. It will help to "stretch out" your years – to slow or reverse your aging no matter what your chronological age.

#40
INSTANT TENSION RELEASE: EASY QIGONG LESSON

You will love this great tip on how to immediately free yourself of emotional tension! This is done using a simple and very effective Qigong "patting" technique. And it only takes a few seconds to do.

Here are your step-by-step instructions:

1. Stand up straight with feet shoulder-width apart.

2. Make "soft" fists with both hands.

3. Inhale through your <u>nose</u> as you raise fists to the lower chest.

4. Start gentle, but firm, patting alternating fists on lower chest, then moving fists upward on the chest.

5. As fists reach top of chest, exhale through the <u>mouth</u> with an audible sigh as you pat downward while slightly "collapsing" your posture.

6. Next, straighten up, inhale and repeat the process 3-4 more times.

Use this routine after most any stressful situation to help release the tension you are experiencing. It's a handy tool to have available at all times.

#41

THE LAW OF THE GARBAGE TRUCK

We wish we created this story, but we didn't. And we don't know who did, but we love the message and wanted to share a version of it with you. It says so much.

Some time ago while in a large busy city, we caught a taxi and headed out to a meeting. We were driving in the right lane when suddenly a black car sprung out of a parking space right in front of our cab. Our taxi driver slammed on his brakes, skidded, and missed the other car by just inches!

The driver of the other car opened his window, whipped his head around and started screaming and swearing at us! Our driver simply responded with a big smile and a friendly wave at the guy! So we asked him, "Why did you just do that? That knucklehead nearly destroyed your car and sent us to the hospital!"

This is when our taxi driver taught us what we now call, "The Law of the Garbage Truck."

He explained that many people are like garbage trucks. They run around full of garbage, full of frustration, full of anger, full of stress, and full of disappointment. As their garbage piles up, they need a place to dump it and sometimes they'll dump it on you. He said not to take it personally. Just smile, wave, wish them well, and move on. Don't take their garbage and spread it to other people.

The bottom line is that grounded and happy people do not let garbage trucks take over their day. Life is much too fleeting to let this happen. So, love the people who treat you right and even save some love for the ones who don't. Life is ten percent what you make it and ninety percent how you react to it!

Have a garbage-free day!

#42
AN HOUR EARLIER

Here's a practical suggestion to stretch your day and get you off to a great morning start. It is simply getting up an hour earlier! Yes, yes, we know sleep is important and we encourage 7-8 hours nightly. But we've discovered years ago that there are good reasons to get out of the sack sooner than you are doing now if at all possible.

Eight Reasons for Rising an Hour Earlier:

1. Gives you a head start to your day – bonus time to fully wake up, clear your head and help get you in a feel-good, less anxious, and rested mood.

2. Empowers you with private time for some introspection – Reviewing all you are grateful for, calming the mind, writing, journaling or just sitting in relaxed contemplation or meditation.

3. Serves as the perfect time to do some stretching, exercising, walking/running, and/or Qigong.

4. Enables you to eat an unhurried nutritious breakfast, as opposed to the on-the-run variety.

5. Affords focused productive time to think through, fine-tune and plan the rest of your day.

6. Allows additional time for grooming and dressing so you look and feel better.

7. Gives you a jump-start to tending to your children, spouse or partner.

8. Helps to avoid traffic and crowds on the way to work, school, social gatherings, volunteer commitments and events of all kinds.

While it's impossible to utilize all of the items in the above list, choose how you want to use this "extra" hour in your day. It can work well for most anyone, whether you're a student, working or retired.

#43

ABOUT GMOs

Genetically Modified Organisms (GMOs) can be simply defined as any plant or animal that has had its DNA modified or altered through genetic engineering.

While there are those who say that GMOs are harmless or even good for you, we personally choose to avoid them. Our research indicates that plant seeds have been injected with chemicals that have been linked to many serious diseases including cancer.

We believe that what we eat should be natural and not changed chemically or in any other ways. Many countries throughout the world have actually banned the growing of GMO crops.

Not only are GMO crops grown in the US, the labeling of these foods is not mandatory. However, many food companies have recently chosen to label their products "Non-GMO Project Verified." You can find their small emblem with a butterfly on many products. This is especially important with items containing soy or corn since about 90% of the corn and soy grown in the US are GMO.

We encourage you to do your own research on GMOs.

#44
FISHING

Here's a story we heard when we started living in Thailand for extended stays. It contains a great lesson about how much we need in our lives.

A group of tourists arrived in a tiny Thai fishing village. One of them complimented the local fishermen on the good quality of their fish and asked how long it took to catch these fish.

"Not very long," they answered in unison. "But why didn't you stay out longer and catch more, asked the tourist?"

The fishermen explained that their small catches were sufficient to meet their needs and those of their families. The tourist continued, "But what do you do with the rest of your time?"

"We sleep late, fish a little, play with our children, and take siestas with our wives. In the evenings, we go into the village to see our friends, have a few drinks, play the guitar, and sing a few songs. We have a full life."

The tourist interrupted, "I have an MBA from Harvard and I can help you! You should start by fishing longer every day. You can then sell the extra fish you catch. With the extra revenue, you can buy a bigger boat."

"And after that?" one of the fishermen asked.

"With the extra money the larger boat will bring, you can buy a second one and a third one and so on until you have an entire fleet of trawlers. Instead of selling your fish to a middleman, you can then negotiate directly with the processing plants and maybe even open your own plant.

You can then leave this little village and move to Bangkok. From there you can direct your huge new enterprise."

"How long would that take?"

"Twenty, perhaps twenty-five years." replied the tourist.

"And after that?"

"Afterwards? Well, my friend, that's when it gets really interesting " answered the tourist, laughing. "When your business gets really big, you can start buying and selling and make millions!"

"Millions? Really? And after that?" asked the fishermen.

"After that, you'll be able to retire, live in a tiny village near the coast, sleep late, play with your children, catch a few fish, take a siesta with your wife, and spend your evenings drinking and enjoying your friends."

"With all due respect sir, but that's exactly what we are doing now. So what's the point wasting twenty-five years?"

So, the moral of this story is: **Know where you're going in life. You may already have enough of what you need. You may already be there! Simply enjoy.**

#45

A LAUGHING MATTER

We've all heard that "laughter is the best medicine." Now medical research has confirmed that approaching life experiences with optimism, humor, smiles, and laughter is, in fact, very good for your health.

People with a positive outlook tend to ward off diseases better than those who are inclined to be more negative. We're certainly for using laughter over pills any day!

Noted researchers Dr. Lee Berk and Dr. Stanley Tan from Loma Linda University in California have reported the following stunning findings:

Health Benefits of Laughter:

1. **Reduces Hypertension** (blood pressure) – this can result in lower risk of stroke and heart attack.

2. **Lowers Stress Hormone Levels** – reducing mental stress and anxiety results in less harm to the physical body.

3. **Enhances Immune System Performance** – laughing activates T-cells (immune system cells) that help defend against discomfort and disease.

4. **Improves Heart Health** – laughter serves as a cardio workout getting your heart pumping and burning up calories.

5. **Eases Pain** – laughing releases endorphins to help relieve pain.

6. **Increases Overall Well-Being** – laughter can increase your overall sense of feeling good, happy and in harmony.

"Don't take life too serious because you'll never get out of it alive!" is one of our favorite sayings. We believe in not taking <u>ourselves</u> too serious, as well.

This kind of light, not-so-serious spirit is one of the most important keys to staying young, regardless of your age or station in life. From smiles to snickers, to giggles to big belly-laughs, it's all good medicine for us – totally free with no co-payment! ;)

#46
FIVE TERRIFIC TOOLS
FOR HEALTHIER LIVING

Here are five practical tools that we personally use to enhance our health and well-being.

Essential Oils. These are a highly concentrated adaptation of the natural oils in plants which include their fragrance as well as their healing properties for both physical and emotional wellness. Essential oils have been used throughout history in many cultures. We mix lavender and frankincense oils in a mister (diffuser) in our bedroom all night. It has aided us in our sleep. It is also said that essential oils have an uplifting effect on the spirit and helps in relaxation. Essential oils can also be used on the skin or ingested for a variety of possible benefits. We advise you to do your own research on the types and qualities of various essential oils and enlist your doctor's permission prior to using.

Earthing (Grounding) Mats/Sheets. These are used to transmit energy from the earth into our bodies. We use earthing mats daily while barefoot when working at our desks or sitting on a couch. We simply plug our mats into a grounding outlet. It is a good substitute for walking barefoot directly on the earth. The benefits include increased energy, pain reduction, improved sleep patterns and lower stress levels. Another way is to get a grounding sheet for your bed. Check all of this out on the internet and happy earthing!

Reverse Osmosis Water System. Our personal research verifies that while progress has been made in purifying our drinking water in America, there remains a number of toxins and contaminants still approved for consumption in many areas. These may include lead, chromium 6, carcinogens, pesticides/herbicides, and fluoride. Because of this, we chose to use a countertop reverse osmosis water purification system for our home that removes or substantially reduces all the toxic chemicals in our tap water. In our opinion, this is far more effective than other types of water filters (i.e. refrigerator or pitcher). We believe that this helps prevent illness and promotes a healthier lifestyle. Drink lots of good water every day!

Salt Lamps. We use a salt lamp in our bedroom, but many folks have these placed throughout their homes. They are said to help purify the air by increasing negative ions to counter the positive ions given off by electronic devices. Salt lamps are known to help calm allergies, enhance sleep, boost blood flow, and raise serotonin levels. Salt lamps work for us, but do your own investigating.

Dust mite-Proof Mattress & Pillow Covers. We recently switched from conventional mattress and pillow covers to hypoallergenic ones. Even though we have no known allergies, we wanted extra protection from any possibilities of dust mites, allergens, bacteria, mildew and mold while asleep. We've been happy with this decision and encourage you to consider doing the same if you haven't already. There's a wide range of qualities, features and prices so check these out online or at a retail store.

Consider these terrific tools to grow healthier and younger!

#47
THE "PERFECT" GAME!

Here's a great tip that comes from our son, Rich. It is from his and our daughter, Robin's, best-selling book, "Living the Law of Attraction."

Growing younger in mind, body, and spirit and attracting more and more wonderful life experiences can be achieved when you "Go with the Flow" of life. You handle <u>every</u> situation that comes your way with a positive outlook and an optimistic attitude. This is what we refer to as rowing easily downstream, instead of battling upstream.

This philosophy empowers you to stay in the easy blissful journey of a stress-less happy life. It is accomplished by continually turning lemons into lemonade … negatives into positives.

You can do this by playing The "Perfect" Game: There is just one rule – **no matter what happens, you declare everything to be PERFECT!**

- You get a flat tire —"PERFECT, I'll walk … I could use the exercise."

- Your feelings were hurt by someone – "PERFECT, I will use this person as a teacher who just taught me a life lesson on how <u>not</u> to act toward others."

- You didn't make the sale – "PERFECT, I will attract a better customer and a bigger transaction. This experience will make me get better at what I do."

- It rains on your day off —"PERFECT, I will stay home and read or meditate or do some things I've wanted to do."

- The boyfriend dumps you —"PERFECT, I am confident I will attract a new and improved one!"

Always be tuned into this and catch yourself being negative about anything...and change your focal point to a positive one.

You will notice that "bad" things will happen less frequently and when they do you simply will not be affected as much. When you turn perceived negatives into positives, as a way of life, you will experience more happiness, inner peace, and vitality as a result.

Play The "Perfect" Game every day starting now!

#48
HOW TO PREVENT FALLS

This piece may not be what you think! It's literally about breaking bones and how to guard against falling! In just the past few weeks we heard about 9 people who fell and broke a leg, ankle, shoulder, wrist, ribs, etc. This can happen at any age, but it tends to be more prevalent as we get older. **Reports indicate nearly a third of elderly Americans suffer from falls each year. About half of them require hospitalization.**

Here's A Handy Checklist for Avoiding Falls:

1. ____ **Be focused and avoid rushing.** So many accidents occur because we are not concentrating or are in too much of a hurry. As a result, we walk into something or trip on the edge of a rug and break a toe or a rib or worse. So stop the rushing, be focused and always move carefully in and around the house.

2. ____ **Hold on!** If necessary, have grab-bars and handrails installed in bathtub, shower, next to a toilet and on stairways.

3. ____ **Go non-slip.** Be certain you have a non-slip surface in your bathtub and shower. Also, use non-slip mats to prevent falls on slippery wet floors in your bathroom, kitchen, front and back porches, and stairways.

4. ____ **Repair or remove any and all tripping hazards.** These can include loose carpets, throw rugs and clutter, especially in hallways and on stairways. Make sure your home is well lit, and be sure to have a night light in the bathroom.

5. ___ **Don't take chances.** Be extra cautious when using step-stools or ladders, walking on sidewalks and in the yard. Place items that are frequently used within easy reach so that you won't have to use a step stool.

6. ___ **Sit down.** If you are not as flexible as you used to be, sit down when putting on or taking off slacks, underwear, pajamas, etc.

7. ___**Avoid wearing ill-fitting clothing.** Of course, you want to be comfortable at home, but baggy clothes can sometimes cause a trip and fall. Choose clothing that doesn't bunch up or drag on the floor. Wear shoes or non-slip socks and slippers.

8. ___ **Out and About.** Be especially mindful when you are out walking, hiking (use a hiking stick/pole), gardening or bike-riding. Use caution at all times, wear safe proper footwear, avoid taking risks and stay within your comfort zone to avoid accidents and falls.

9. ___ **Practice good balance.** It's a good idea to do things to improve your balance. Consult your doctor about this and consider taking a qigong (chi gong) class for this purpose.

Accidents can happen to anyone but let's do our best to avoid them whenever possible.

#49

THE PERFECT BRUNCH - PECAN-CRUSTED FRENCH TOAST RECIPE

Totally Delicious! And Totally Healthful as it contains NO eggs or dairy products. This one Fran uses on weekends and when entertaining friends. They never leave without asking for this recipe.

Here's what you need:

- ⇒ 1 1/2 cups non-dairy milk (soy, almond, rice or coconut)
- ⇒ 3 T cornstarch
- ⇒ 1 t cinnamon
- ⇒ 6 T whole wheat flour
- ⇒ 1 cup finely chopped pecans
- ⇒ 6-8 slices whole grain bread
- ⇒ Maple syrup

Here's how you put it together:

Whisk together milk, cornstarch, cinnamon, and flour in a bowl. Place chopped pecans on a plate. Heat frying pan. Dip bread in milk mixture and then press one side of bread into pecans. Cook on both sides and transfer to a plate.

Serve with maple syrup and fresh berries or bananas.

There probably won't be any leftovers, but if there are, it tastes great reheated.

Mmmmm, soooo good!

#50

EASY QIGONG LESSON: WAKE UP YOUR ENERGY!

Here's a great way to start every morning! It's called Qigong Energy Patting (or Tapping) designed to awaken your energy or Qi (pronounced "Chee") so you can enjoy a day full of vitality.

Just follow these step-by-step instructions:

1. Stand straight with feet separated shoulder-width apart and knees slightly bent. Body soft and relaxed. Center yourself quietly for 15-60 seconds breathing naturally in and out of your nose.

2. With soft fists start patting firmly and briskly (alternating fists) on your lower back at the tailbone and then up the spine as high as comfortable. Repeat this up and down pattern several times.

3. Next, with open hands pat down from your lower back onto your hips and then pat down the outside of your legs down to your ankles, around your ankles and continue patting up the insides of your legs until your torso is upright again.

4. Now keep patting on the upper thighs and down the front of your legs as far as you can bend, then pat around the ankles and pat up the back of the legs to a standing position.

5. Standing upright, extend your left arm forward with the palm facing down and elbow bent slightly. Reach your right hand across your chest and pat on your left shoulder blade, then onto the shoulder joint, then continue patting down the outside of the arm, wrist, and fingers. Next turn the left palm up and pat the

palm and continue patting up the arm and on the top of the shoulder area.

6. Repeat #5 on the right side. Extend right arm forward with the palm facing down, etc...

7. Finally, again with soft fists, pat firmly on your chest area, alternating fists for several seconds.

8. End by standing quietly and relaxed with eyes closed and arms at sides just for a minute or so, breathing easily in and out through your nose. Feel both the calmness and the energy that is the essence of Qigong.

Once you learn this simple routine, it only takes a few minutes to get your body revved up with energy ... like putting gasoline in your car! Give this a try. Then make it a habit.

#51
PAIN and SUFFERING STORY

2,600 years ago the Buddha was attributed with teaching that, "Pain is inevitable but suffering is optional." We will all experience pain from time to time, but we can choose whether to suffer or not. And there will be no suffering (stress) if you can elect to "LET GO!"

This idea is exemplified beautifully in the following story that we learned from one of our wisdom teachers in Thailand some time ago:

Two Buddhist monks, one senior and one novice, were returning to their temple at the end of the day. It was the monsoon season and it rained heavily that day. The river that they needed to cross to get to their temple had risen quite a bit.

As they arrived at the river bank, they saw a young woman standing there, looking quite anxious. They exchanged glances and the senior monk understood that the young lady was afraid of crossing the river. Without any words spoken he approached her and gently picked her up in his arms, crossed the river and put her down on the other side. She bowed in gratitude and respect before heading toward her home.

The novice monk was troubled by the actions of the senior one knowing it was not allowed for a monastic to even touch a woman. Out of reverence and respect, he stayed quiet, although upset. The two monks continued walking toward their destination. Silence persisted for a good few hours before it was broken by the junior monk.

"Please, may I ask you a question," he said.

"Yes, of course." The elder one replied.

"According to our code of conduct, we are not allowed to touch a woman, correct?"

The senior monk said, "Yes, indeed, that is correct."

After agonizing over this for a while longer, the younger one finally asked, "So, how come you carried that young woman across?"

"I simply lifted someone in need. I believe I did the right thing" the elder one replied. "Besides, I put her down hours ago ... while you are still carrying her!"

The moral of this story is that most people do not want to "let go," and many others, do not know how to do it. It boils down to one choosing to "let go" or not. If not, the suffering, tension, worry, anger, and stress will continue. Which option will you choose?

#52

BE THE CHANGEMAKER

We strongly believe in the adage that **helping one person might not change the whole world, but it could change the world for that one person.**

Now more than ever, people need people. Now more than ever, we need "change-makers" to come to the aid of people in need. Now more than ever, we need to be more aware of those around us who we may be able to assist and make their situation more tolerable.

We're not talking about protesting, demonstrating or any form of violence against the oppressors of others. Instead, it is about taking direct action and being the light to those living in darkness.

This requires us – regardless of age, ethnicity or station in life – to tune-in and turn-on to the feelings and needs of those living in poverty, fear, or oppression. This can include people who are experiencing or are vulnerable to discrimination, bullying, gender bias, hostility, deceit, and human trafficking.

We need to open ourselves more to reach out to them, engaging them, listening to them and most important, taking some action to change their plight and ease their burden. Acting on behalf of the disadvantaged is the highest of virtues. Make this a daily goal.

Also, share your experiences with others. Persuade friends, family, faith communities, businesses, and organizations to do as you are doing. Being a changemaker sets an example for others and can spread exponentially.

Remember that you may not be able to change the world, but you have the power to change someone's life for the better. Your being a changemaker can and will influence the future of our society. So, **always do your best to help alter the direction of humankind for the better – one challenge, one situation, one person at a time.**

#53

TAKE CHARGE OF YOUR HEALTH

Here's some common-sense advice on maintaining and improving vitality and good health at ANY age.

We learned long ago to think and act in terms of working together with a doctor to **prevent** disease rather than waiting until you become sick to take action! We would encourage others to do the same.

Unfortunately, for generations, most people have been dependent on their doctors for making health decisions for them. They went to the doctor when they were sick and were prescribed a pill as a cure. For a very long time doctors were considered infallible, almost "worshiped" and not to be challenged. Sadly, many people still feel this way. They get sick, go to the doctor, are given drugs and often expensive tests and treatments. So now the idea of paying for more of these "health services" has become routine.

But does this classic cycle really work? Are people more healthy? We don't think so. **It seems to us that people are not living longer ... they are dying longer!**

Just look around. Diabetes is rampant. Heart disease is more prevalent than ever. We all seem to know at least one cancer sufferer. Orthopedic issues affect more and more of us. Obesity is an epidemic. And doctors' waiting rooms are jammed!

At the same, time drug sales and prices continue to skyrocket! Medical tests are almost automatic. Surgeries have escalated and the use of dangerous chemicals and radiation is commonplace and accepted. What is going on here? Maybe doctors now have less time to spend with patients? Maybe there's a lot of care guessing going on? Maybe there are profit motives? Maybe pharmaceutical and insurance companies are impacting our health care. Maybe it's partly because doctors have little or no knowledge about nutrition or alternate approaches to curing disease.

The good news is that there are alternatives for you to this fruitless and frustrating "health merry-go-round!" Start on this new path by taking control of your own health and not always solely depending on mainstream MD's to tell you what to do. Engage your primary doctors about their views on non-traditional ways to treat as well as stave off discomfort and disease. This goes back to prevention.

If your physician appears to know little about treatment and prevention of illness and pain through a healthy lifestyle, you may want to seek out a doctor who does... one who will work together with you to optimize your health and energy. This also means you may have to personally research and discover new and different health methods and providers.

Look for medical doctors who use words like "integrative," "preventive," "functional" or "alternative" in their descriptions. Also, consider consulting a naturopath, nutritionist, chiropractor, acupuncturist, or a doctor of Chinese Medicine. As an additional adjunct, look into qigong, tai chi, yoga, healing touch, reiki, and other healing arts.

We are absolutely not suggesting you just "dump your doc" tomorrow! But we believe in finding a good balance between mainstream and alternative medical practices. We think it is wise to explore and be open to new possibilities for managing your health instead of letting one doctor control it for you.

#54

INVISIBLE PEOPLE

You can "make someone's day" and enrich your own by doing small but meaningful acts of kindness to people you encounter who seem to be invisible to most.

A smile and friendly "hello" to food servers, store clerks, grocery baggers, delivery men/women and other usually unnoticed fellow humans can make a big impact.

"Humanizing" telephone customer service or support representatives by asking how their day is going or complimenting them will be a welcome change from their daily barrage of complaints and criticism.

Acknowledging and speaking with office cleaners, receptionists, repair people and other everyday "invisible" folks makes them feel good. And so will you. Make this an every day habit!

#55
EUDAIMONIA! Huh?

Eudaimonia. ([Pronounced "you-da-monia"). Yes, it's a new word for you to think about. It is from Greek philosophy and refers to a state of contentment one feels as a result of taking the right action. It means achieving the best conditions possible for yourself, in every sense—not only happiness, but also virtue, morality, and a meaningful life.

It can manifest itself through the rising of your inner spirit that is experienced by doing a good deed or selflessly helping someone. It is said to enhance your health, vitality, and prosperity, as well.

Eudaimonia should be viewed as a goal to become a better person and to fulfill our potential as human beings. Aristotle wrote a lot about this idea and we know it still works wonderfully today.

We think it wise to learn from him by setting your intention of achieving Eudaimonia starting now ... regardless of your age or station in life. Write "Eudaimonia" on a sticky note and place it on your bathroom mirror as your daily reminder. Begin to cultivate this state of inner fulfillment today by doing good things for others.

Who wouldn't want to live with a consistent "feel good" spirit!

#56
HOW TO LIVE A MORE
STRESS-FREE LIFE

Stress is something we all can do without, especially as we age! It can adversely affect us mentally and physically. It cuts into our personal peace and happiness. With stress comes negative emotions such as anger, disappointment, fear, and worry. It can wear us down and make us sick.

For a lot of us stress can worsen as we age. Our lives are ever-changing – maybe more now than ever before. New challenges and issues arise. New circumstances come into play ... from family and friends to relocating your home to financial considerations to health problems and more. Stress can bring heartache, loneliness, and depression. So, the first and maybe the most important method of staying young is to do away with as much stress in your day as possible. Here's how ...

Start to incorporate this very transformative idea NOW to lower your stress levels fast and begin reversing your age! It's called Acceptance.

Acceptance is simply recognizing the truth of the moment. From small situations like getting a flat tire on your car to major events like a death of a loved one ... stuff happens and you cannot control them. These are life's realities ... good things and bad... and you must understand "It is what it is," like it or not.

Here are our Five Steps for Reducing Stress Through Acceptance:

Step One: Do not deny or resist any circumstances that flow into your existence. When you resist, the stress will persist...and often get worse.

Step Two: Simply accept each of life's experiences in every instance. You know that you cannot rewind the clock and change what occurred.

Step Three: Handle each circumstance to the best of your ability. Refrain from over-reacting. Just go with the flow!

Step Four: Acceptance is a simple idea, but it's certainly not always an easy one to carry out. So, keep this idea "front of mind" by heightening your awareness of it.

Step Five: Then begin accepting situations or conditions that arise with calmness and objectivity.

You will get better and better with this practice as you keep doing it. Your stress levels will be lowered and it won't get the best of you!

#57

"HOW DO YOU GET YOUR PROTEIN?"

We get this question A LOT! Mainly because people know we advocate eating a plant-based diet for good health and vitality.

Some people ask this because they don't know that there are many sources of protein other than consuming meat and dairy products. But most ask because they wisely want to reduce or eliminate meat and dairy and are concerned about consuming enough protein.

So, here's our answer in this list of some of our favorite plant-based foods that provide plenty of protein and fiber, as well:

- Leafy Green Vegetables – Spinach, Lettuce, Kale, Arugula, Chard, Collards, etc.
- Lentils
- Beans – Black, Kidney, Pinto, Lima, Garbanzo (chickpeas), etc.
- Quinoa
- Milk – Made from Soy, Almonds, Coconut, or Hemp
- Peas – Green and black-eyed
- Artichokes
- Seeds – Chia, Hemp, Sesame, and Pumpkin
- Oatmeal
- Tofu, Tempeh, and Seitan
- Broccoli
- Edamame

- Green Beans
- Asparagus
- Raw Nuts – Almonds, Pecans, Walnuts, Cashews, Brazil, etc.
- Nutritional Yeast
- Peanut Butter

There are loads of flavorful, easy and creative recipes online and in health-oriented cookbooks that incorporate these and other protein-rich foods.

Eat Well = Stay Young!

#58

KEEP YOUR MIND OPEN
... A STORY

A long time ago, there was a wise Japanese Zen master named Nan-in. People from far and near would seek his advice and ask for his wisdom. Many would ask him to teach them and enlighten them. He seldom turned any away.

One day he received a university professor, an opinionated man used to authority and getting his own way. "I am a highly educated person and have come to see if you can teach me the way to enlightenment," he said in a somewhat curt manner.

The Zen master smiled and said that they should discuss the matter over a cup of tea. When the tea was served the master poured his visitor a cup. He poured and he poured and the tea rose to the rim and began to spill over the table. Finally, the visitor could not restrain himself any longer and shouted, "Enough. You are spilling the tea all over. Can't you see the cup is full and will hold no more?"

The master stopped pouring and looked at his guest. "You are like this tea cup, so full that nothing more can be added. Come back to me when the cup is empty. Come back to me with an empty mind."

We love this story! It's a good reminder that we don't "know it all" and that we should be humble and keep our minds open to make room for learning new ideas as well as the views of others.

#59
TRANSFORMING UNWHOLESOME HABITS

We all have some habits that are not at all beneficial. These negative habits can be caused by low self-esteem, fear, worry, boredom or other deeper factors. We feel that recognizing unhealthy habits and replacing them with positive alternatives will result in less stress and more happiness.

We started brain-storming some prevalent unhealthy habits people have these days. See if you can identify with some of these just as we did ... then make a strong effort to substitute them with new beneficial habits.

Eating Unhealthy Food – Sweets and meats and too many cheats! Change this unhealthy habit into a plan for a healthy eating lifestyle consisting of a whole grain, mostly plant-based diet. Tips to do this include reducing temptations by ridding your home of all processed and unhealthy foods. Reduce or, better yet, eliminate consumption of all animal products. Use natural (no chemicals) sugar substitutes like stevia. Eat until you are 80% full. Choose raw vegetables to snack on in place of chips or cookies. Avoid fast food restaurants. Lose weight, become more energetic, look and feel good!

Monkey Mind – This involves worrying or being fearful about something in the future. Also, being angry or upset about something in the past. Two unproductive habits that create tension. So when you become aware that your mind has wandered, gently take your focus back to the present moment. Repeat this simple regimen as needed. This will train your mind to be here and now. Mindfulness is a key to happiness.

Complaining, Criticizing and Judging Others – These are harmful, negative and often knee-jerk behaviors. So when you catch yourself knocking or faulting someone, change your thoughts to the good qualities about the person. Also, be cognizant of your whining about something. Then, when this happens, transfer your thoughts to the many things for which you are grateful. Replace the negatives with positives as your new habit.

Too Much Sitting – If you find yourself sitting too much at work or in front of the TV, there's an easy fix. It's called "Get Off Your Butt and Move!" You can transform this unhealthy sitting habit at work or home while reading or studying by setting your watch or computer timer every 30 minutes to get up, stretch and walk around. Do the same for watching the tube – at every commercial get up, stretch and walk around till your show resumes. Also, make a plan to walk, run, or bike for at least 20 minutes every day, preferably in the morning. Sitting can be as dangerous as smoking! Make the change.

Procrastination – There are ways to stop constantly putting off or delaying tasks until later. Break this habit by dividing a project into parts and doing one at a time. Create specific deadlines. Encourage friends and family to help you accomplish your to-do goals. Avoid over-complicating things. Remember KISS – Keep It Simple Silly!"

Spending Money You Don't Have – Impulse shopping or over-shopping can be a disastrous habitual behavior. Invoking new spending habits is essential if you are overspending. Start now by creating a weekly budget including income and living expenses so you know your spending limits. Cut up credit cards. Use only cash. List only the items you need when shopping. Shop at thrift shops, buy groceries at discount no-frill stores, watch for sales and stock up. Find free things to do. Consider shopping with a friend who will help curb your spending money beyond your means.

There are loads of other unwholesome habits from nail biting to constantly interrupting people to excessive cell phone usage. The following ideas can be used to transform most bad habits into good ones.

Five Tips For Breaking a Bad Habit:

1. Be tuned-in to your specific negative habits. Catch yourself!

2. Make a plan to substitute a good habit in place of a bad one.

3. Eliminate whatever "triggers" are likely to set off the unwholesome habit, for example, having a bowl of candy nearby.

4. Engage a friend to be your "accountability partner" to report to regularly and help keep you on track. Also, consider teaming up with another person with the same unproductive behavior so you support each other.

5. Tell others of your intention to break certain bad habits and that you would appreciate their understanding and support.

Start now and always do your best ...

#60
WORLD'S GREATEST HOMEMADE GRANOLA RECIPE

Most commercial cereals are loaded with sugar and unpronounceable ingredients! So we want to share with you a healthy and nutritious granola recipe given to us by a friend.

Ingredients:
- ⇒ 6 cups Non-GMO rolled oats (not quick cooking or instant)
- ⇒ 2 cups mixed raw nuts and seeds such as sunflower, chopped walnuts, pecans, almonds, cashews, sesame seeds, hemp seeds, flax seeds and/or pumpkin seeds
- ⇒ 1 cup dried unsweetened shredded coconut
- ⇒ 1 tsp ground cinnamon
- ⇒ Dash of sea salt
- ⇒ 1/2 to 1 cup of maple syrup or to taste
- ⇒ 1 cup chopped dried fruit (we use golden raisins)

Instructions:
1. Preheat oven to 300 degrees
2. Place a 9x13 inch baking pan over one or two burners on low heat. Add the oats and cook, stirring occasionally, until oats begin to change color and become fragrant, 3-5 minutes
3. Add the nuts and seeds and continue to cook, stirring frequently, for 2 minutes. Add the coconut

and cook, stirring for 2 minutes more. Add the cinnamon, salt, maple syrup and stir. Place in oven. Bake for 20 minutes stirring once or twice during that period.

4. Remove from oven, add dried fruit, stir, and cool on rack til granola reaches room temperature.

5. Transfer to sealed containers. We use three one quart Mason jars.

Great for breakfast with fresh fruit and yogurt or as an occasional snack right out of the jar!

#61

UNHEALTHY "HEALTHY FOODS!"

"What the large print sayeth,
the small print taketh away!"

Fact: Today's food packaging can easily fool most consumers. The wording on the package front cover can influence buying habits. Food and drink companies are good at being tricky and using words and phrases to entice shoppers into thinking they are eating healthy, even though they are not being totally honest.

Beware: Look out for eye-catching bold words or phrases such as, "All Natural," "Fresh," "Gluten-Free," "Naturally Sweetened," "Light," Multi-Grain," "Healthy," "Energy Foods and Drinks," and "no sugar" or "reduced sugar" or "no added sugar." They appear to be healthy products, but they are often very misleading.

Read: If you want to assure yourself that you are truly buying healthful food, don't just count on what the front label is saying. Be certain to read the back and sides of the package. Check the list of ingredients, the nutrition facts and the per serving size which can be very small to further confuse consumers. Note that items listed on ingredients labels are in order of weight. The ingredient that weighs the most is listed first.

Advice: Stay away from products containing fructose, corn syrup (or high fructose corn syrup), saturated fats, hydrogenated or partially hydrogenated oils, trans-fats, palm oil, "white," processed, shortening, artificial sweeteners, artificial colors (blue, green, red and yellow), and MSG. Also avoid nitrates, preservatives (Sodium Benzoate, Potassium Benzoate, and Butylated

Hydroxyanisole – BHA) and other "chemical-sounding" words that you can't pronounce. If you don't recognize the ingredients, either will your stomach!

Understand: Processed food is unhealthy food. Any food that is dehydrated or contains added chemicals is processed. It's not in its natural state. Sadly, these foods now compose an overwhelming percentage of the average diet in the U.S. The FDA is supposed to protect consumers, but in our opinion, they are not and do little to check deceptive food labeling. So, we must become smarter shoppers and make truly healthy food choices on our own.

Conclusion: Don't be tricked into buying unhealthy "healthy foods!" Don't trust the large print and be sure to read the small.

#62

HOW TO KEEP THE MIND SHARP

We talk a lot about taking charge of your physical health, but it's equally important to purposefully maintain your cognitive well-being as part of the aging process. This centers on the ability to think clearly, comprehend new ideas and remember what you've learned.

First, understand our view that there is a connection between mind and body and that the health of one can affect the wellness of the other. This requires your ongoing awareness and caring for your overall health, eating nutritious foods, being physically active and remaining socially engaged.

Second, constantly be tuned in to how your mind is functioning and do things to keep your mind sharp. Here are some ways that work for us:

1. Undertake ongoing intellectually stimulating activities like volunteering or hobbies.

2. Continually learn some new skills to improve your thinking abilities like cooking with new recipes, becoming more tech-savvy, taking or teaching a class, writing articles on subjects that interest you, and practicing qigong.

3. Keep your mind active by reading, playing word games, and researching topics of interest on the internet.

4. Avoid being "dumbed down" -- by your television, listening to too much news, becoming 'creatures of habit,' not getting enough sleep, and finding yourself being bored.

5. Clear your mind by making time to simply sit quietly once or twice a day and meditate on a single-focused point like your breath.

It's important to continually care for the mind as well as the body.

#63

THINGS

We live in a time where we can buy more things than ever before. We can buy beautiful clothing and dazzling jewelry. We can buy cool cars and even ones that drive themselves. We can buy devices to which you can ask most any question, and they will answer! We can buy fancy coffee drinks, ultimate cellphones, and caviar from Russia. We can buy in stores and we can buy online. We can buy things anywhere, anytime! We can be instantly gratified.

People even brag about their shopping! "Look at all the 'things' I bought today!" It becomes their identity. Buying stuff is who they are and is what seems to make them happy. The more "things" they get, the better they feel!

Really? Is this good for us? Is shopping one of the most important activities we do? Does it enhance the quality of our lives? Does it really make us happy and secure?

We sure don't think so! Buying another "thing" may provide a temporary boost. But this will usually not last long and so the "high" becomes a "low" and this leads to a need to get yet another something. In our view, this desire for "things" is a negative, unproductive, and harmful habit that should be changed.

We suggest reflecting on this. Become aware if you or a friend is giving too much attention and effort to accumulating "things." Then ask yourself if these "things" may be serving as substitutes for more meaningful life factors like love, relationships, harmony and good health. Or could it be a way to overcome boredom or feed a shopaholic addiction?

Whatever the reason, **the method for altering this behavior can be achieved by focusing not on what you want, but on what you <u>have</u>.** It's about appreciating the essentials of life and being grateful for them.

This can be a process, so if and when the desire to buy some "thing" arises, re-focus on all you already have and take a pass on shopping. The more you do this, the easier it becomes.

And most important, remember – **The best things in life are not things!**

#64
DON'T BE TOO QUICK TO JUDGE

There's a story about a father and his 20-something year-old son. They were looking out the window of a moving train.

The son says "Dad, look! The trees are moving backward!"

The dad smiled. But a young couple sitting nearby were whispering to each other about the son's seemingly childish comments.

The son then blurted "Dad, look up, the clouds are moving with us!"

The couple could not hold back any longer and said "You should take your son to a good doctor. He needs help!"

The dad smiled again and said…"I did just that. And we are just coming from the hospital. My son has been blind from birth. And today is a great day! His eyes now see for the first time!"

The message here is obvious. Everyone has a story. To judge a person for any reason, especially without knowing their story, says more about your character than that of the person you are judging. It is self-centered egoistic behavior that serves no good purpose. So, be aware of your tendency to judge others. When judging thoughts arise, simply stop them. Judge less, love more and enjoy the feeling of an opened heart.

#65
HOW TO BOOST YOUR IMMUNE SYSTEM

Understand that you don't get permanently well unless you permanently change the way you live. So to stay healthy at any age, it is important to build a strong immune system. The following is a list of things you can do to help boost your immunity to disease:

- Include more whole grains, fruits, and vegetables in your diet, and significantly reduce sugar and saturated fat.

- Exercise regularly. Some suggestions would be daily walking, qigong, yoga, and biking.

- It is recommended to get 7-8 hours of sleep each night. The cells in your body repair themselves during sleep.

- If you drink alcohol, do so in moderation. No smoking. No drugs.

- Maintain a healthy weight.

- Wash your hands thoroughly and frequently to avoid other people's germs.

- Ask your doctor about supplements that boost your immunity. We personally take 2,000 mg of vitamin C daily and 5,000 IU of D3 weekly. If we feel a virus coming on, we increase the amount of both until we feel better.

- Keep a positive outlook! We all know people who are sure that they will get the flu every year and . . .

they do! Instead, be positive that you will stay healthy. And you will!!

- Having solid relationships with family and a good social network is good for you. Studies show that people who feel connected to friends – whether it's a few close friends or a large group - have stronger immunity than those who feel alone.

A strong immune system is the key to preventing discomfort and disease. Work on it every day!

#66

REVIEW THE MAGIC

Every night, before you go to bed, either talk about or write down all the magical things that happened that day. At first, you may not feel there was any magic in your day, but when you start to really think about it, you will see that there were many miraculous and touching moments.

The magic can be a bird at your feeder, a rainbow after a downpour, a call from an old friend, a handwritten letter in the mail, a nice word from a co-worker, a pleasant greeting from a stranger, a compliment on your appearance, a delightful dinner, or just feeling really good all day.

Let's not take our days for granted. Take a few minutes to recognize and appreciate all the wondrous things, big or small, that we encounter daily. It will make you happy and you'll sleep better, too.

#67

TIPS TO AVOID DANGEROUS EVERYDAY CHEMICALS

On an average day, most people are exposed to hundreds of cancer-causing chemicals – in our homes, in our food, in the environment – everywhere! We can't eliminate all of them but we can certainly **reduce our exposure** to many of them. Following are some of our suggestions:

Cosmetics – Commercial cosmetics are loaded with cancer-causing chemicals and dyes that are absorbed through our skin. We strongly suggest you choose cosmetics with mineral-based pigments and natural oils. Choose soaps and shampoos **free of synthetic fragrances and chemicals** such as triclosan which has been found in animal studies to alter hormone regulation. Substitute commercial shampoo for natural brands such as Nature's Gate.

Hair Color – Most brands of hair color used in beauty salons or purchased for home use contain dangerous ingredients. Try switching to a safer alternative such as Herbal Tint.

Deodorant vs. Antiperspirant – Years ago scientists determined that antiperspirants containing aluminum may cause breast cancer. Stay away from products that contain parabens and all ingredients with 'PEG' in their name. Natural deodorants such as Kiss My Face are safer alternatives.

Air Fresheners – Many brands contain chemicals that are harmful to your home environment. Anything you inhale eventually ends up in your bloodstream. Plug-in scents or synthetically scented candles may contain chemicals called phthalates which have been linked to reproductive problems. Instead, choose candles made with essential oils. Consider a safer room spray like Citrus Magic, as well as simply using baking soda and white vinegar for absorbing odors.

Toothpaste – Many brands contain carrageenan or fluoride - both associated with the higher risk of cancer. Look for natural brands that do not contain either or, better yet, make your own with coconut oil and baking soda with a few drops of clove essential oil!

Sunscreen – We've all heard how important it is to protect ourselves from the harmful rays of the sun by slathering or spraying our bodies with sunscreen before going outdoors. Recent research, however, has shown the opposite to be true. Most sunscreen products contain cancer-causing chemical ingredients such as oxybenzone, octinoxate, retinyl palmitate, and fragrances. Also, sunscreens can work to block needed immune booster vitamin D from being absorbed. Avoid spending too much time in direct sun. But when you are in the sun, keep your skin moisturized with natural oils, such as coconut oil.

Cleaning Products – Eliminate products that use chemical ingredients such as phthalates and chemical surfactants. Better yet, go simple and safe by just using natural products like baking soda, Borax, and mixing vinegar, lemon and hot water to clean your home without toxins.

Plastic Bottles and Food Containers – Everyday plastic water bottles leach dangerous chemicals into your water. Avoid at all costs! We personally use Hydro-Flask bottles as a safer alternative. It's unhealthy to heat foods in plastic containers as they can release chemicals that seep into your food. Use glass containers for heating food.

Insecticides and Herbicides – If the purpose of these products is to kill pests or weeds, you can bet the ranch they contain chemicals that are harmful to humans.

Fortunately, you can purchase natural and organic pest and weed control products from companies like Buhach and E.B. Stone. Also, Boric acid works as a natural insecticide and household vinegar can eliminate those weeds.

Other everyday products to avoid include laundry and dish detergents, non-stick cookware, antibacterial products, plastic shopping bags, perfumes and the list goes on and on. It's important to be your own advocate for healthy product choices. Read labels to easily spot hard-to-pronounce chemicals, research safe alternatives on the internet, and reduce exposure to cancer-causing chemicals in and around your home.

#68

BRING PEACE TO EVERY MOMENT

How can we make our planet a kinder, happier and more peaceful place? It all starts with each of us. To make the difference we want to see, as individuals, we need to convey a sense of harmony and calm to every social interaction, situation, and experience.

It is not always easy, but it is possible. This means avoiding confrontation, staving off arguments, communicating calmly, and acting to reconcile differences with people of differing views and temperaments.

It's been said that only when a mosquito lands on your private parts that you realize there is always a way to solve a problem without aggression, force or hostility!

Bringing peace to every moment every day is the answer. It's doing our job to make the world better.

#69
ATTACHMENT

Attachment is the root cause of one's suffering. Being personally attached to a particular outcome, situation, person, or thing is the condition that causes stress, frustration, and anxiety. Attachment occurs when we want life situations to be a certain way. We have this need to control and/or alter what is happening because it doesn't conform to our desires.

Attachment means clinging to your ideas and expectations. It is the "I want" that creates agitation or aggravation when things don't go as you wish. It is this ego-driven behavior that results in the absence of inner peace.

Non-Attachment is the antidote for Attachment. So, it's important to first **be aware** of your wanting or clinging to something. For example, you are upset because you want your daughter to go to college, but she prefers to travel for a year. Or you voted for a politician, but he lost the election and you remain in an ongoing state of disbelief and disappointment. Maybe you saw a flashy car advertised on TV and you develop a craving for one just like it even though it's costly and your present car runs well.

Second, it's a matter of **fully accepting the reality of life** to which you and everyone is a part. And going with the ever-changing flow of the Universe. This includes giving up ill-conceived habits and self-serving notions that block the path to happiness.

Third, understand that peace, contentment, and freedom arise when we **take action** by making a deeply concentrated effort **to retrain the mind** to process life as it is and not as we want or think it should be.

If your goal is to grow younger and healthier in mind, body and spirit, Non-Attachment is an important key.

#70
86,400

This is our version of a short narrative we heard long ago:

What if you had a bank that automatically deposited $86,400 in your account every morning? However, what was left in the account after your withdrawals did not carry over to the next day. So, naturally, you would want to withdraw the entire amount every day!

Actually, we all have a bank like this. It's our "Time Bank." Each morning you receive 86,400 seconds. Each night it writes off whatever you don't use wisely. So any wasted time does not carry over to the next day. You can't borrow time or use another person's time. The time for that day is simply gone!

We are fortunate to have time. It costs nothing and we can decide what we want to do with it. We can spend it but we cannot keep it. And once it is spent, we can't get it back. Time is our most valuable asset. It's a gift we receive every morning. But when tomorrow comes, this gift disappears.

So, we must ask ourselves how do we want to spend our time each day. We can waste it or we can use it wisely. The choice is ours.

#71

SIGNS YOU'RE WALKING ON THE RIGHT PATH

Are you experiencing any of the following symptoms? If so, do not be alarmed. No need to call your doctor. Things are simply flowing in the right direction for you!

- Frequent intense episodes of gratitude and joy.
- A sharp decline in re-living moments that make you angry.
- Putting space between what you experience and how you react.
- An increased inclination to "let go" of stressors that arise.
- A loss of interest in confrontation or conflict.
- A gradual decline in expectations.
- A heightened awareness of your own behavior.
- Losing the ability to worry about things that haven't happened.
- Feeling happy for no particular reason.
- A sudden decrease in judging others or one's self.
- An obvious tendency to live moment to moment.
- The cessation of trying to change others and just changing yourself.
- Making more and more lemonade out of lemons.
- A definite leaning towards accepting experiences as they are without resistance.

- Taking full responsibility for your actions. No more blame-games.

- Doing acts of kindness for friends and strangers alike.

- A dramatic reduction in complaining, criticizing and controlling.

- A tendency to watch life's drama unfold, rather than be in it.

- Just sitting quietly while calming the mind.

- An increased desire to serve the needs of others.

- A growing feeling of inter-connection with everyone and with nature.

- Becoming more and more open to new ideas, things and people.

- An increased ability to find enjoyment in every moment.

- Accepting life as it is rather than how you want it to be.

- An overwhelming feeling of unconditional love for all beings.

#72

HOW TO INCREASE YOUR ENERGY

We are frequently asked how to increase energy levels. To us, energy is fuel for the body, just as gasoline is for your car. People tell us that they often run out of gas in the afternoon and that fatigue sets in after dinner so they just plop down on a couch and watch TV before going to sleep!

We're happy to share some things we do to keep our energy levels up and to maintain a youthful vitality.

First is Food – We get energy from healthy food. Fresh fruits and a few raw nuts for breakfast. We suggest you do not eat a big lunch – soup and/or salads would probably be good for you to overcome afternoon malaise. For dinner eat to just 80% of being full. In all meals strive to reduce or eliminate the "whites" - sugar, salt, flour and dairy products. Cut out fatty foods and soft drinks. Simple. Clean. Energizing food.

Second is Movement – Exercise energizes us. We advise a morning routine that includes some stretching followed by a brisk walk for at least 20 minutes. An after-dinner stroll helps food settle and gets the energy circulating through our bodies.

Third is Sleep – Getting a good night's sleep is needed for sufficient energy. We try to get at least 7-8 hours of sleep nightly.

Fourth is Qigong – (Pronounced "chee gong") is our secret weapon for increasing energy. Qigong means "energy exercise" and is an ancient Chinese system of health care. It consists of a series of slow gentle movements and postures. It enables us to cultivate, circulate and store energy. It's fun and easily learned. 129

Qigong keeps us energized and helps reverse aging. We strongly encourage you to research Qigong and find a teacher you like. It can change your life, just as it has changed ours.

Talk to your doctor about these ideas. Once you get the go-ahead, start incorporating these methods to build and maintain your energy. In short – eat right, keep moving, sleep well and play Qigong.

#73

THE FLOATING NURSING HOME

Not long ago we went on a two-week cruise for some relaxation and recreation. Soon after we boarded the ship we saw that this sailing was geared for older passengers. Well, we never saw so many canes, walkers, scooters, and wheelchairs other than in a nursing home!

For the most part, our fellow passengers looked unhealthy and the majority had "Dunlaps Disease." That's where your stomach "done laps" over your belt! We quickly learned that most did not get the connection between what they ate and their health. Frequently we joined others for dinner and the main topic of discussion at the table was usually about people's ailments and diseases. It was almost a game of one-upmanship – who had the most afflictions! We even saw a woman openly inject herself with insulin after eating a big steak. She followed that with a dessert of ice cream and cake! Toward the end of the cruise, a ship's officer told us that three people had actually died onboard during the cruise!

While we understand that cruising may be the best way for folks with health issues to travel, this experience served as a "wake-up call" for us. It reinforced our personal dedication to living a healthy lifestyle and doing all we can to PREVENT DISEASE. It also fortifies our belief that getting older does NOT have to mean getting sicker.

So, please join us in eating more whole-grains and plant-based foods and exercising daily. We're confident this gives us the edge to meet our life goal of "dying young – as late as possible." It's worked well for us so far.

#74

PROTECT YOURSELF FROM SCAMS

We've heard from some of our readers of their concerns about being scammed. So, we've listed our top ten tips that will go a long way to avoiding swindles, hacks and identity theft. We urge you to heed these simple suggestions and stay safe.

1. Place your home and cell phone numbers on the Do Not Call registry at 1-888-382-1222 or www.donotcall.gov.

2. Never give out important numbers like your social security number to anyone who calls you.

3. Throw away unsolicited lottery or sweepstakes mailings.

4. Avoid products that claim to be miracle cures.

5. When you need work done on your home, ask friends for recommendations.

6. Never agree to invest in or buy something you don't fully understand.

7. Research unfamiliar charities before you donate.

8. Don't carry your social security card in your wallet or print your social security number on your checks.

9. Shred outdated tax records, credit card applications, old financial statements, etc.

10. Limit the number of credit cards you carry. One card is enough for most people.

Follow these tips and always be on guard!

#75

WHO ME WORRY?

Worry is one of those habitual emotions that can immobilize us. It's being trapped somewhere in the future. Worrying about something that hasn't happened yet is a matter of not being in the present moment but in a future moment.

We view worrying as the mind rehearsing the very things that you don't want to happen! This is non-productive behavior, a waste of time and energy, and certainly a creator of stress.

So, what's the fix for worry? First, you need to be aware when worry arises. Second, when you catch yourself thinking about something that may or may not occur, gently re-focus your attention to what's happening now.

We're betting that 80%-90% of what we worry about, never comes about! Just be here.

#76

AVERTING DEMENTIA and ALZHEIMER'S

As most of us know, dementia and Alzheimer's Disease are among the greatest concerns as we age. Dementia is a class of brain disorders that result in difficulties like remembering things, thinking clearly, making decisions, and controlling emotions. Alzheimer's disease is one of those disorders.

The Bad News: One out of three elderly Americans dies of Alzheimer's or another dementia. Alzheimer's Disease is the sixth leading cause of death in the U.S. Nearly every minute of every day someone in the U.S. will be diagnosed with AD. It kills more people than breast cancer and prostate cancer combined. More than 5 Million Americans have Alzheimer's.

The Good News: Recent research indicates that Alzheimer's and other forms of dementia are preventable! Studies are starting to show that lifestyle choices and proper management of other health conditions can help delay or even avert dementia. Experts are saying that adopting healthy lifestyle habits is the key.

The Link: There is now substantial evidence linking brain health to heart health. So, risk factors for the heart are also now being considered as the same risks for brain disorders like AD and dementia. These include poor diet, lack of physical activity, obesity, high blood pressure, stress, among others that damage the heart and blood vessels. This also means that the same lifestyle changes that reverse heart disease can also prevent or delay AD and vascular dementia.

Reversing the Risks: This takes a determined effort to replace unhealthy habits with healthy ones.

Diet – Heart-healthy eating is very important as it may also help protect the brain. This means eliminating eating saturated fats from meats, fish, eggs, oil, dairy products plus sugary and salty foods. Instead eat more of a whole-grain, plant-based diet including fresh fruits and vegetables, nuts, whole wheat pasta, brown rice and whole grain bread. This type of diet also helps to maintain and even reduce weight.

Smoking and Excessive Drinking – Do whatever it takes to STOP! Join a support group, consult your doctor, make a plan and stick to it.

Physical Condition – Keep moving by daily walking, biking, stretching, exercising, playing Qigong and yoga. These activities provide good blood flow to the brain and promote new brain cell growth.

Mental Condition – Use your brain by exercising it to stay mentally sharp. Do this by taking a class, doing puzzles, playing games, and learning computer skills, as examples.

Social Interaction – Make a concerted and ongoing effort to keep a circle of friends, spend time volunteering, take lessons at local learning centers, stay active and socialize daily.

Sleep Well – Strive for 7-8 hours nightly. Keep your bedroom dark and quiet. Remove any electronic devices such as mobile phones, computers, and clock radios from the bedroom. Exercise during the day and take a walk after dinner to help with sleep. Turn off TV and computer about one hour before retiring. Consult with your doctor for some natural sleep enhancers such as melatonin.

Safety First – Protect yourself from falling and bumping your head. Make sure your home has clutter-free floors, non-skid rugs, and non-slip surfaces especially in bathrooms and kitchen. Install handrails where needed and remove wires and cords that can cause tripping. Always wear a car seat belt and a helmet when biking or playing sports.

Get your doctor's approval before changing your current health regimen including diet and exercise.

#77

THE STARFISH STORY

There are many versions of the tale. You may have heard some version of this story, but we would like to share our short adaptation, as we love the message:

One early morning an elderly gentleman was walking along the beach that was littered with starfish washed ashore during a storm the night before. When he came to each starfish, he would pick it up and throw it back into the ocean. He had been doing this for a long time when a young woman approached him and said, "Old man, why are you doing this? Look around, you can't possibly save all the starfish. You can't begin to make a difference!"

The man then bent down, picked up another starfish and flung it back into the sea. He looked deeply into the eyes of the woman and replied, "Well, I made a difference to that one!"

The woman pondered what just happened and she joined the wise man in throwing the starfish back into the ocean. Soon others saw them and did the same.

This story is a wonderful reminder to purposefully take time to make a difference – big or small – in the life of someone. And magically, this kindness seems to spread exponentially.

#78
ONE-WAY CONVERSATIONS

Have you ever had a one-way conversation? That's when you meet someone, often for the first time. In an attempt to get to know each other better, you plan a get-together. The chat usually starts with some small talk and then onto subjects like hometowns, work, interests, activities, family and so on.

But as the conversation progressed or after it ended, you realize that you asked all the questions and got their answers, but it wasn't reciprocal. So you learned quite a lot about the other person or couple, but they learned little if anything about you. It was very much one-sided.

There is a valuable lesson here. It is to view the other person as your "teacher" and to keep your ego in check whenever you are engaged in any conversation. **It's wise to talk less about yourself and focus more on others to be sure that you are not the cause for a one-way conversation.**

#79
LIFE ASSESSMENT CHECK-UP

We think it's a good idea to occasionally tune in and turn on to how things are going for you in life. Striving for a life of health, harmony, and happiness is worthwhile. But at times we don't have the right balance that we seek. This self-evaluation can lead to focusing on parts of your life that could be improved and then get you going in the right direction to fix the issue(s). Here's the path ...

Step One

Write down the following **Eight Facets of Life** and thoughtfully rate each of them in terms of your satisfaction from 1 to 10 (highest). For example, Health = 5 and Career = 8. Take your time with this.

1. Health
2. Spirituality/Personal Growth
3. Financial
4. Family and Friends
5. Volunteering in Your Community
6. Recreation
7. Romantic Relationships
8. Career or Education

Step Two

For each of the Eight Life Facets, ask yourself, "How are things working for me?" Then create a list of things happening that are of concern and/or challenging in each category. For example, Family and Friends, "I don't have enough contact with my grandchildren."

139

Step Three

Make specific goals to improve your situation in each Life Aspect within a specific time period – 24 hrs, 72 hrs, or one week. Example, Volunteering, "I will call Meals on Wheels tomorrow and commit to delivering food to the needy on a regular basis." Then act to accomplish each goal you set for yourself.

Step Four

Get "an accountability partner" to help you and to whom you report your actions and progress on a planned regular schedule. For example, in the Financial Aspect ask a friend to assist in reducing your personal spending and start a savings program.

Also, it can be productive and fun to share this Life Assessment Check-Up with others and you can be mutual "accountability partners" to each other.

We suggest doing the Life Assessment Check-Up every few months. It can help you to be the best version of you!

#80

HOW TO TRANSITION TO A HEALTHIER DIET

There is great power in the food we eat. Some foods can make us healthy. Some can make us sick.

It is estimated that approximately 80% of the food sold in supermarkets today did not exist when many of us were children. Unfortunately, most of these "new foods" are unhealthy refined products loaded with chemicals, sugar, and fat. They can cause serious and chronic disease.

Whether you are in poor health and would like to get well or are in good health and would like to stay that way, we recommend adopting a whole food plant based diet as much as possible. Not only will it make you healthier, it will also benefit the planet and the welfare of animals!

Here's a simple step-by-step guide to get you going in the right direction:

Step One: Make a commitment. Dedicate yourself to eating a more healthy diet. Start now and avoid procrastination!

Step Two: Make a plan.
Determine your **motivation** for a dietary change – personal health and well-being, environmental concerns, or animal rights.

Next, choose the **type** of diet.

- ○ **Vegetarian** – eliminate eating all beef, pork, poultry, seafood, and fish.
Or
- ○ **Vegan** – don't eat anything that had a mother! This would be only plant-based foods and

whole grains – no eggs or dairy products including milk, cheese, yogurt, ice cream, or butter.

- o **Note** – If you have been diagnosed with a serious illness, we encourage you to get serious about a vegan diet as soon as possible. More and more studies show that a whole food plant-based diet can reverse most disease.

Step Three: Do a pantry and refrigerator make-over! Give away your present supply of meats, poultry, and fish.Do the same with all processed, sugar-laden foods, including white bread, desserts, snack-foods, cereals, soft drinks and products with high fructose corn syrup that you have in your home. This shows determination and gets you started with a clean slate.

Step Four: Shop for healthy foods. Replace these items with lots of fresh vegetables, fruit, and whole grains (pasta, rice, bread). Include a few nuts plus seeds in your daily diet.

Step Five: Cooking. Change your view of cooking from a chore to a hobby. When you cook, get your family involved and fix meals that look good and taste great. There's a wealth of vegetarian and vegan recipes online and in designated cookbooks for delicious nutritious meals and snacks. As a bonus, you will find you will be spending less money on food.

Step Six: Engage family and friends. Encourage others to improve their eating habits. Share ideas, recipes and support each other.

Start now and change your life forever!

When making changes in your diet or exercise regimen, it is advisable to first consult with your doctor.

#81

HOLIDAY HEALTH AND HAPPINESS

Holidays are times for celebration, togetherness, and joy. Yet many find this time of the year to be challenging, stressful, even depressing. Most of us are somewhere in between - having fun in some situations and pressure in others.

So, we would like to share with you some practical tips and reminders to help make your holiday season the Best One Ever!

SEVEN STEPS TO A WONDERFUL HOLIDAY SEASON

1. GO FOR BALANCE AND HARMONY

- **Manage Your Time Wisely.** During the often hectic holiday season, it is important to balance your time for family, social and religious events, helping those in need, as well as private "down time" for yourself. Plan ahead and refrain from trying to please everyone and accept all invitations. Make up for any holiday bail-outs by making a date for after the New Year.

- **Do Everything In Moderation** ... including eating, drinking, partying and shopping.

- **Avoid Rushing.** Purposefully slow down, take some "deep breathing breaks" to release any emotional tension, and pace yourself through the day.

- **Be With People You Love.** Attend functions that you are sure about and where you will enjoy folks who are in your life. Also, invite friends, family, and co-workers who are alone during the holidays to spend time with you.

- **Do What Makes You Feel Good.** The holiday season can be complicated with so much going on, but it's important that you take care of yourself during this time. Decompress by sleeping-in once or twice, reading a book you've been meaning to for awhile, treating yourself to a massage or the spa to de-stress. Do some things that make you relaxed and happy!

- **Express Gratitude.** It is good for the spirit to reflect daily on all you have for which you are grateful. Take time to contemplate and internalize your appreciation for family, friends and loved ones with whom you celebrate the season. And in a quiet moment, tell them how grateful you are to have them in your life.

2. PRACTICE LOVING-KINDNESS

- **Lead With Your Heart.** This time of year is an especially good time for being patient, compassionate and caring toward others. More people feel stressed out during the holidays and it can be an emotionally challenging or extremely lonely time for many. Tis the season for a heightened awareness of the feelings of others and to act as a calming influence whenever possible.

- **Be Kind to Yourself.** Why not use the holidays as a reminder to lighten up on yourself. Be less self-critical. Have more self-respect. Believe more in your self-worth and care less what others may think. Focus on your good qualities. Love yourself as you are.

- **Renew Old Friendships and Family Ties.** What better time to make a conscious effort to call or visit old friends and family members with whom contact has dwindled or even stopped. Do more than a Facebook post or a text message. Make this fun and friendly. Everyone benefits!

- **Focus on Forgiveness.** Reach out to end grudges and reconcile differences with others. This is big! Use this special time of the year to take the initiative to "patch up" past disagreements with people who you may have wronged or who may have wronged you. It doesn't matter. This can take courage, but it usually is well worth the effort. Making peace with others can be a highlight of your holiday season!

3. ACCEPTANCE MAKES THINGS EASIER

- **Understand That Some Things Will Not Go As Planned!** Seasonal stress for you and/or others is to be expected. Flights will be delayed. Turkeys will be burned. People will say things that may be hurtful. How one reacts to these situations will shape how the holiday will be remembered.

  This tension affects some people more than others. You can be one of those who can handle adversity instead of crying in your eggnog. The secret is to accept the reality of what's happening, whether you like it or not, and deal with it the best you can.

- **Manage Expectations.** A good holiday strategy to employ regarding family and friends is to keep your expectations low. Be realistic about people, accept them as they are, and know that you cannot change them. You risk facing big disappointments when you anticipate or hope someone will react a certain way or if things don't go as expected. Forget about being the perfect host when entertaining guests. Don't hesitate to ask others for support and help when preparing for a holiday event.

- **Handle Family Friction.** The holidays can amplify problems in already strained relationships for example if you have critical parents, hard-to-please children, or moody siblings. Tensions can easily escalate fast, especially if you are spending longer than usual periods of time with family.

  The fix for coping with these tense situations is to prepare yourself in advance for some heated situations, stay in control and keep out of the drama that's unfolding before you. Just be the observer to what's going on and don't jump into the fire. It's also a good idea to get away and take time for yourself, even if you are hosting visitors.

- **Tradition!** To many of us old holiday customs and traditions are the most wonderful parts of the season. But, sorry, sometimes things change and plans are altered. The result is that the holidays don't look, feel, smell or taste as we remember them or how we think they should be. So, it's good to prepare yourself to be open to new ones and be flexible and accommodating. Just go with the flow and remember you have the power to make it a good time even if it's not like it used to be.

4. BE GENEROUS

- **Help People In Need.** This is the perfect time to put some cheer into the lives of needy people by volunteering at a local charity, doing a series of acts of kindness, and also financially supporting your favorite charities.

- **Start a Gifting Project.** Organize family and friends to forgo or minimize the usual gift-giving to each other and pool the money to benefit folks who need it more. Remember – people who do good for others tend to live longer and healthier lives!

- **The Best Things In Life Are Not Things.** Think about how you can give more of yourself and your time rather than giving gifts of more clothes, toys or other "things." Examples would be treating others to events with you (concerts, lectures, seminars, classes), taking a joint trip somewhere (near or far), or just enjoying private time together (sharing meals, hobbies, personal skills).

5. TAKE CARE OF YOUR BODY

- **Maintain a Strong Immune System.** Do your best to stay healthy and energized to maximize your holiday enjoyment. This means retaining your regular healthy habits and not letting the holiday season sway you in another direction.

- **Eat Right.** Yes, you will see more cakes, cookies and other sugary foods everywhere. Temptations will abound! Do your best to make healthy food choices like eating more plant-based foods, less meats, less dairy products, and yes, less sugar and fat. If you are a vegetarian or vegan, our advice is to simply stay on course.
  If you can't resist a "totally worthwhile cheat" once in awhile, then go for it! But avoid over-indulging and putting off good eating habits until next year. Consuming more alcoholic

beverages during the "jolly season" is also a temptation to avoid. In all situations, use good judgment, common sense, and moderation.

- **Be On The Move.** Resist forsaking your exercise during the holiday period. Be sure you do an every-morning routine of at least stretching and walking/jogging. Make time for it! If you have guests or are visiting others, suggest to them to work out with you. Also, if you regularly attend a fitness class, continue it throughout the season if at all possible. Stay in shape, recharge your energy and have fun!

- **Sleep and Rest.** Getting a good night's sleep is important to keep up your energy level during this busier-than-usual time of the year. Taking rest breaks during the day is a good idea. Just sitting quietly or meditating daily is relaxing and helps control holiday stress.

6. MINDFULNESS MATTERS

- **Be Here and Now.** During the holiday rush, the more you can be connected to and live in the moment, the more joy you will experience. And it's the ideal time to share this joyous feeling with people around you and then out to the Universe.

- **Let Go!** The holiday time can revive unpleasant memories and resulting stress. It is wise to let go of the "ghosts" of past holidays. If and when these thoughts arise, you have the power to change the mind, to turn your thoughts to happy ones and detach from the past. The same applies to your dreading future holidays. Change what you think about and stay out of the unpleasant past or future.

- **Depression, Loneliness, Grief.** The holidays can be particularly trying for people suffering from mental and physical illness and for those who are lonesome or grieving. We all are expected to be happy at this time of the year! However, this is often the opposite for those who are sick, depressed or feel alone.

  If you fall into this category or know of a family member who does, it helps to be open and honest about one's depressing feelings and emotions with family members <u>ahead</u> of holiday visits. This will help take pressure off having to appear to be cheerful and happy even though one is not. Family members should reach out to each other early on and work to understand and be sensitive to how everyone really feels and decide together which seasonal traditions and plans work best for all.

- **Optimism Helps.** You have the choice to take a positive outlook on the holiday season or a negative one. If you anticipate a stressful holiday season experience, you have a very good chance that your negative thoughts will come true! Pessimistic thinking can trigger your body's stress response, just as a real threat does! Conversely, an optimistic outlook will help you cope with challenges that come your way.

7. BE DIFFERENT

- **Adopt-a-Family.** Plan ahead with family and friends to host a needy family for the holidays complete with good food, gifts for all and meaningful interaction that hopefully will continue far beyond the season.

- **Try an Interfaith Holiday.** Combining Christian, Jewish, Muslim, Hindu and other holiday faith traditions can be wonderful, educational, and delicious, too! Make an effort to bring together people from various religions. Ask them to be prepared to teach others about their holy days and bring traditional food and drinks to share. This can become one of your most meaningful holidays ever!

- **Consider Abandoning Old Customs.** Discarding old customs can be a good strategy if you seek a totally new holiday experience. This idea can be particularly comfortable for those who may be non-religious, lonely, grieving, or who feel their family is too dysfunctional to cope with. Experiment by developing your own new traditions with others who may feel the same as you.

- **Embrace Diversity.** How about organizing a festive themed event based on another culture! Maybe a Mexican Thanksgiving feast with a variety of tacos, burritos, and enchiladas? Or how about a Greek Christmas? Hey, maybe an Irish-style New Year's Eve party? Have guests bring information on the themed country to share. Try to include people from that chosen culture as your holiday guests.

- **Celebrate in Another Country.** Discover new and different holiday customs and experiences by traveling abroad during this time. This takes some research and preparation, but it can result in a fabulously memorable holiday. Plan ahead and go for it!

May you and your friends and family enjoy every holiday season – filled with peace, happiness, good health, and love!

And may you continue using many of these ideas throughout the year.

#82

EIGHT WORLDLY WINDS

The Eight Worldly Winds is one of our favorite Buddhist life lessons. The Winds are four pairs of opposite conditions. One we are drawn to and the other we find repulsive. But just like a sailboat on the sea, we are sure to experience both sides through changing and uncontrollable circumstances over life's journey.

The Eight Worldly Winds are:

Pleasure and Pain – We crave Pleasure and hate Pain.

Praise and Blame – We get hooked on Praise and we loathe Blame.

Dishonor and Fame – We abhor Dishonor and cling to Fame.

Loss and Gain – We don't want to lose what we have and we want what we don't have.

Pleasure, praise, fame, and gain all make us feel good. This is what we desire and want it to continue. Our egos can inflate with fame, we can become too complacent with pleasure, rely too much on others with praise, or become overly comfortable with gain. However, this can backfire when conditions change and the Winds shift, causing instability and suffering to arise.

Conversely, pain, blame, dishonor, and loss do not feel good. We can become absorbed by our pain, our confidence and self-respect can erode from dishonor, guilty feelings arise with too much blame, and loss can lead to much sorrow. Here the inevitable changes also develop and the Winds stir things up so we lose clarity and again we become stressed.

Such is life! But there exists a practical day-to-day protection for this. In Buddhist terminology, it's called **Equanimity. This means maintaining a state of observing and accepting each of the Eight Winds without attachment to any of them while fully understanding they are all impermanent.** It is the ability to see what is unfolding in one's life but not getting caught up in it. It involves "keeping your cool" even in difficult situations, remaining calm and even-tempered without aversion to any situation.

Equanimity can be one's safeguard against stress and suffering. And it's the basis for wisdom and freedom. **Understand that the good times don't last and neither do the bad times.** So avoid getting attached to any of the ever-changing Eight Worldly Winds and don't get blown off course.

#83
TIPS & TIDBITS - EVERYDAY THINGS WE DO

Here's a random series of practical things, mostly little but important to us, that we personally do to stay young in body, mind, and spirit. While some of these tips may not be scientifically proven, they have helped us stay healthy and happy. Hopefully, some will resonate with you.

1. Primarily shop the perimeter of the supermarket for healthier non-processed foods.

2. Have a Himalayan salt lamp in our bedroom to improve air quality & reduce allergens.

3. Drink lemon water first thing every morning to be more alkaline.

4. Park in the far end of any parking lot and walk to our destination.

5. Eliminate dryer sheets and fabric softeners because of cancer-causing chemicals.

6. No soft drinks of any kind, including "diet" drinks and "energy" drinks."

7. We say "N-B-D" a lot. It stands for No Big Deal. So whenever a life challenge arises, big or small, we accept it, handle it, and move on.

8. Limit exposure to negative news stories.

9. Use "grounding" mats (aka "earthing" mats) to connect us to the energy of the Earth. This helps reduce pain and inflammation and promotes healing.

10. No electronic devices in our bedroom to eliminate health-harming electromagnetic fields (EMFs).

11. Use natural toothpaste without carrageenan or fluoride or make toothpaste from coconut oil, baking soda and a couple drops of clove essential oil.

12. Use stairs instead of elevators or escalators whenever possible.

13. Limit bread (whole grain) to one meal daily.

14. Totally avoid fast-food restaurants (except for bathroom breaks when traveling!)

15. Use only chemical-free natural room fresheners and deodorizers, and cleaning supplies.

16. Use lavender essential oil in air diffuser in the bedroom during sleep.

17. Utilize countertop reverse osmosis water system to reduce exposure to fluoride and other impurities.

18. On Tuesdays, we cleanse our bodies and manage weight by eating only fruits, nuts, and vegetables: fresh seasonal fruit plus a few raw nuts for breakfast; fresh garden salad for lunch; and mixed green salad, baked potato or vegetable soup for dinner. Use only oil-free dressings on salads.

19. Usually, we limit dining-out to just one meal a week.

20. Meditate in a quiet place daily – even if it's just for a few minutes.

21. Use mattress and pillow covers especially made to protect against dust mites.

22. Avoid casein, a cancer-causing ingredient, found in dairy products & some non-dairy substitutes.

23. A short easy walk after dinner helps settle the food.

24. Use natural makeup, hair color, and deodorants.

25. Absolutely no plastic water bottles. Only double-layered insulated glass bottles by Hydro Flask.

26. Stevia instead of sugar.

27. Practice Qigong every day for energy, relaxation and to build up the immune system.

28. Grow some of our own vegetables.

29. Go to bed about the same time nightly and get 7-8 hours sleep.

30. Avoid all canned tomato products. Buy only those in glass jars or boxes. Fresh preferred, of course.

31. Less TV and internet is best for us.

32. Choose organic foods whenever possible.

33. Avoid carrying cellphones close to our skin or in pockets. Use the speaker instead of holding the phone close to our faces. No Fitbits and other similar "wearable" devices that emit EMFs.

34. Drink green tea (hot or cold) daily.

35. Wash all fruit and vegetables in water to which baking soda has been added.

36. Avoid negative people and situations.

37. Wine at 5:00 pm is a tradition!

Which of these ideas are you already doing or will institute?

#84

MEDITATION ... IT'S NOT WHAT YOU THINK!

We like keeping the idea of a daily meditation quite simple. And it is. We learned this idea from one of our wisdom teachers. Just go to a quiet place, sit comfortably and simply "watch your breath." Do nothing else. No mantras, no counting, no visualizations, no thinking about anything – just watch your breath.

You can observe your breath as it comes in and out through the nostrils or the gentle movement of your belly with each inhalation and exhalation. Nothing more. No thoughts. Just sit and watch your breath without judging it, forcing it, or altering it. If thoughts come to mind, gently re-focus back to watching your breath. Easy and soft.

Some tips: Try to commit to setting a specific time or two during the day to do this breath-watching. Make it a habit. You may want to start with a five-minute sit. Then add another minute or two as you are comfortable doing so over time. Advance up to 15-20 minutes in quiet stillness. Also, use this meditation anytime you feel the need to escape the frenetic pace of the day. It's a wonderful tool to clear the mind, re-charge the body, and lift the spirit.

Oh, and don't <u>think</u> about doing this daily sitting. Just do it! Start now ... it can change your life!

#85

TEN WAYS TO HAVE A LONG HAPPY MARRIAGE or PARTNERSHIP

Speaking from experience, we believe that a great marriage or enduring loving relationship can be the most important factor for living a happy life. When there exists a strong natural unconditional bond between two people, life does not get better!

Here's are the ways that have worked for us for the past 55 years and to which we still abide:

1. Marry or partner with your best friend. Know what you're getting in advance.

2. Love and accept one another in "as is"condition. Absolute and completely.

3. Take care of each other. In sickness and health and in everything else.

4. Compromise. Whatever the issue make an agreement that satisfies both sides.

5. Add excitement. Continually mix new ideas, adventures, and people into your routine.

6. Communicate. Avoid holding things in. Have no secrets. Share everything together.

7. Team up to make a difference. Create projects to better your community.

8. Pay compliments to each other. Make each other feel good every day.

9. Never become too old for sex! Keep the romance going and do what works.

10. Do not go to bed mad at your spouse or partner. Making up is the fun part.

We think marriage or partnering should be fun, not work. This happens through unconditional love and respect.

Finally, in a pinch simply insist on having the last words to your loved one – "**Yes, Dear!**" Works every time!

#86

LONELINESS

If you have feelings of loneliness at times, know that you are not alone. In fact researchers on this issue estimate that 20% to 50% of us feel lonely sometimes and 5% to 10% feel lonely very often. This can affect people of all ages and backgrounds, including the elderly, people who are socially isolated, and those who are depressed. It can be acute as a result of the loss of a loved one, for example. It also can be chronic.

Loneliness can also affect people who have lots of friends and there are loners who never experience being lonely. Whatever the case, loneliness can be a precursor to ill-health, sadness and withdrawal.

However, there is hope for those who are suffering from loneliness and isolation! We have researched strategies to improve and even overcome this condition. Acting on these ideas requires courage, strength and some risk-taking. But for most, it's well worth it.

Ideas for Overcoming Loneliness:

Start with Small Action-Steps – Engage in light, friendly conversation with people you see in everyday situations.

Befriend Another Lonely Person – This can be uplifting for you and the person you are trying to support.

Volunteer – Serving others who are disadvantaged or need help takes your mind off yourself and can lead to new relationships.

Explore a Faith Community – This can create new friendships and also provide spiritual contentment.

Strive for Good Health – Eat well and exercise daily. Join a gym, walking club, fitness class or similar health-oriented activity to improve your health and meet new people.

Connect With a Pet – Dogs can be wonderful companions. They also can get you out for walks and you can meet other dog-lovers. Cats and other pets can also ease loneliness.

Seek Out Like-Minded People – Most often it's easier to develop friendships with those who have common interests. Look to try groups, clubs or organizations that have that focus.

Pursue a Hobby – Taking on a new pursuit can be enjoyable and lead to socializing.

Take a Class – This can be interesting and is a way to meet new people. Check your local newspaper for a list of lessons being offered.

Strengthen Current Relationships – Take the initiative to invite people to your home or to join you in doing something.

Make Time for Relationships – Make a concerted effort to balance your activities to include getting together with others.

Be Aware of Your Feelings – Do an occasional self-evaluation to determine if you are now open to meeting and connecting with others.

Meditate Daily – Use meditation techniques to help free you from thoughts that may hold you back from engaging with others.

Share Your Feelings – If you know someone you trust and respect, it can be constructive to talk with that person and tell them about your feelings of loneliness. Just talking things out can be helpful and good ideas can spring up to ease your difficulties.

Social Media - Good and Not – Messaging, posting, following and emailing can be fun and is a form of connecting with people and making new friends. But it is not a substitute for in-person discussion and socializing.

Consider Professional Help – If you reach a point of worry and frustration that you are unable to handle and have deep feelings of loneliness, isolation, and/or depression, it may be time to talk to a health professional. Consider one with a cognitive behavioral background.

~ Be sure you consult with your doctor   before acting on any of these suggestions ~

#87

HOW TO DIE YOUNG ...
AS LATE AS POSSIBLE!

For more years than we can remember, we have set an ongoing personal goal of dying "young" in body, mind, and spirit – as late in life as possible! This attitude has worked beyond words for us! We want to share this idea with you in hopes that you will adopt a similar outlook.

The method for accomplishing this goal starts with **setting the everyday intention** of maintaining a youthful vitality and uplifted spirit. Next is to **implement a plan** that enables you to fulfill your intention. This includes:

1. Keeping your **body** healthy by eating well and exercising.

2. Keeping your **mind** sharp by learning new skills, stimulating your brain by reading, playing word games, researching the internet, taking classes or volunteering, and uncluttering the mind through meditation.

3. Keeping your **spirit** high by living out your passions, having a sense of service to others, and a feeling of ongoing accomplishment.

To us "dying young" means living a full, healthy, and happy existence every day. So when our last day on this planet finally arrives, we will have accomplished our goal!

Whether you are 39 or 93 years of age, start living young NOW!

#88

I WANTED TO CHANGE THE WORLD

We love this short essay that was supposedly written by an unknown monk centuries ago. But no one knows for certain about its origin and we've read various versions. Here's our spin on this clear and powerful message.

> *"When I was a young person I wanted to change the world. This was impossible, so I tried to change my country. That didn't work out so I decided to change my home state. No luck. Next, I attempted to change my community. Nada. So, as I aged I thought it wise to just change my family. Failed.*
>
> *So, now as an old person, I realize that I can only change myself. Oh, how I wish I understood this long ago as I could have made a positive impact on my family. Then my family and I could have made a difference in our community. Together our community could have made great changes in our state, and then our state could go on to impact our country and then ... I could have said that I changed the world."*

So the next time you want to change something or someone, look in the mirror first!

#89
LIFESTYLE STRATEGIES

We think it imperative to stop and reflect on the quality and satisfaction with the lifestyle we are leading. Ask yourself, "Can my health and energy be better?" "Do I look and feel as good as I should?" "Why am I feeling so old for my age?" or "Is my life as enriching and enjoyable as I want it to be?" This introspection is valuable and most often leads to some needed changes.

If you are not at the level of health and contentment where you want to be at this time of your life, then it may be time to make some changes. Our Young At Any Age strategies below can serve as your guidelines. It's never too late to change your health and your life – starting now and at any age. It's all up to you and the choices you make.

Eat Well. The most important one first. Change to a style of healthy eating for longevity and great quality of life. This means following a mostly whole food plant-based dietary pattern by reducing or eliminating consumption of meats, fish dairy products, eggs, sugar, fat, salt and processed foods.

Keep Moving! Get off your butt and your "buts." Keep moving. No excuses for not walking, running, biking, or stretching every day. Develop a daily regimen.

Reduce Stress. Participate (not just think about) in alternative stress-lowering modalities like mindfulness techniques, qigong, yoga, tai chi, and meditation. Also, slow down your life's activities.

Connect to a Health-Oriented Community. Seek out and make new friendships and gain the mutual support of like-minded people who desire to be more healthy, happy, and energized.

Have More Fun! Join in and also initiate social gatherings, parties, games, sharing meals together, special interest groups, and celebrations of all kinds!

Benefit from Nature. Get outdoors, walk, picnic, garden, etc. and enjoy the fresh air and natural energy from the environment.

Keep Learning. Attend classes. Learn new skills. Study new ideas and concepts. Expand your mind and your knowledge through education. Consider teaching others and sharing your wisdom as well.

Be Open. Try new things – big or small. Meet new people. Embark on new adventures. Embrace new ideas, places, and ways.

Serve Others. Accomplish this by volunteering at local agencies, aiding friends and neighbors in need, being more generous, doing random acts of kindness, and paying it forward.

Balance is Best. Enjoy a happy and harmonious life by balancing your time and your activities – family, work, social contacts, community, faith, volunteering, and others.

Live Your Life! Act out your personal passions and purpose and enjoy the experience of positive personal growth. Whatever your age, do what you love and love what you do.

Lifestyle modifications can add more years to your life and more life to your years. So ask yourself, "How's my current lifestyle working for me?" Then start to reinvent yourself **NOW**!

Consult your health professional before starting a new dietary regimen and/or exercise program and ask this person if he/she would like to join you!

#90
EASY QIGONG LESSON: SHAKING LIKE A TREE

Qigong, pronounced "Chee-gong," means energy exercise. One facet of Qigong is shaking or vibrating. It is a quick and easy way to wake up your energy and re-charge yourself. We advise your doing this every morning upon awakening and anytime during the day when you feel sluggish, tired, low in energy or have some joint stiffness. The following "Shaking Like a Tree" routine takes only a couple of minutes!

Here are your instructions:

1. From a standing position with feet shoulder-width apart, knees slightly bent and hands down at sides start to bounce your body up/down into your heels and at the same time shake out your wrists for 10-15 seconds.

Note: Continue this light bouncing and shaking throughout this routine, while feet remain flat on the ground.

2. Next, gradually raise both arms overhead while shaking for another 10-15 seconds.

3. Now start to slowly separate arms apart and lower them back down to your sides while continuing to bounce and shake for 10-15 seconds more.

Note: Notice how all the joints – fingers, wrists, elbows, shoulders, hips/waist, knees, ankles – are being exercised as you bounce and shake.

4. Next, transition into a "ragdoll" mode where you shake out your entire body – head, neck, shoulders, hips, etc. Feel "loose as a goose" from head to toe.

Enjoy this full-body shaking for about 15-20 seconds.

Note: There is no right or wrong way of doing this. Just keep shaking, baby!

5. Now gradually slow down the bouncing and shaking and come to a gentle stop. 10 seconds.

6. Finally, close your eyes and stand in stillness with knees bent, arms down at sides and palms facing back. Focus the mind on your palms. Breath in and out of the nose. Soften your body. Feel your entire body come alive and re-charged. 20-30 seconds.

Some of us may feel a tingling or sensation of fullness in the hands which is a sign of Qi cultivation and circulation (this usually comes with daily repetition of this regimen).

This short but powerful Qigong exercise is a highly effective method to instantly energize your entire body. It also works all your joints and tendons, aids in your flexibility, lowers stress levels and can have a positive healing effect, as well.

Get your doctor's approval prior to starting Qigong or any exercise program. The practice of Qigong is our "secret weapon" to optimize health and well-being. If you would like to learn more, seek out a qualified Qigong instructor in your area.

Qi (energy) is fuel for your body, like gasoline is for your car.

#91

THE WAY TO HAPPINESS

Who doesn't want to be happy? We all do! Most of us accept the idea that life is short and that being unhappy makes life stressful. So, we do our best to do whatever we can to make our life a happy one.

We form relationships we hope will make us happy. We buy things that we think will give us instant happiness. We go on vacations and eat foods that are meant to make us happy. We drink alcohol that gets us happy. We take drugs to do the same. We cling to just about anything that we perceive will provide us with the happiness we desire.

But the reality of all this is that these "happiness fixes" we crave do not last very long. This is because of the impermanence of all things and experiences. "I will be happy if I buy a new sweater." "I will be happy if my son goes to college." "I will be happy I if I get this or if that happens." The things that we cling to that initially make us feel happy will quickly make us unhappy once they fade away.

So, we need to understand that there is no "way" to happiness. Being happy is a choice we make. It's getting up every morning and simply choosing to be happy, no matter what! It is a life attitude decision we all have the option of making. It is an emotion that comes from within ourselves, not from other people or experiences.

There is NO WAY to happiness. Happiness IS the way.

And so it is.

#92
A LITTLE ROMANCE...

Whether you are age 38 or 83, adding a touch of romance to one's marriage or loving partnership every day keeps the spark alive and well! Acts of thoughtfulness, tenderness, sexiness, and playfulness will add to the happiness for you and your spouse or partner. Spicing things up is fun, invigorating, inexpensive and strengthens relationships. Make it your intention, starting today.

Here are some romantic ideas that work for us. Pick what you like and create your own!

- Candlelight Dining at Home – Do this together or take turns being "head chef." Makes for a nice once-a-month romantic evening. Both dress-up. Phones off. Do dishes together too.

- Show Your Love in Small Ways – Leave love notes for your spouse or partner, do little things for them without being asked, and whisper in their ear how much they make you happy. You get the idea!

- Devise a Dream Vacation – Enjoy this project together! Plan dates, budget, itinerary, details, and include a volunteering experience during the trip. Unforgettable and romantic.

- Weekly Date Night – Pizza and a movie, take in a concert, play, festival or a local event, and maybe a special dessert afterward. Take turns planning your date nights.

- Massage One Another – Oh yes! You don't have to be an expert. Google it! Do just before bedtime, be gentle, take turns, use a fragrant massage oil. Where could this lead?

- Pack a Picnic – Find a quiet spot, spread a blanket and don't forget the wine!

- Compliments Go A Long Way – Make it a point to compliment your spouse or partner on something every day.

- Take a Class Together – Check with local learning centers and enjoy each other's company by studying and attending lessons side by side.

- Surprise Gifts – Make your spouse or partner's "day" with small gifts from time to time other than birthdays or holidays.

- Day-Trip Getaway – Head off to a nearby small town and stroll the main street holding hands, window-shopping and a leisurely lunch. Perfect!

- Message Your Honey – Why not text or email your loved one once a day just to tell them you are thinking of them and appreciate them.

- Movie and Popcorn Night at Home – Choose old romantic comedies and sit under a blanket together on cold evenings.

- Shake Up Your Routine – Do something different for a change of pace. Go somewhere or do something you both never experienced before. Try a unique new restaurant, get adventurous like zip-lining or hot air ballooning, do something not as adventurous like bowling or roller-skating. Put some excitement into your relationship and keep any boredom out.

- Get Out – Go for slow romantic strolls in a nearby park, do some star-gazing, plant a garden together or take a hike to a romantic place, maybe a waterfall, and bring a light lunch.

- Do Chores Together – Yes, clean the house, wash the car, buy the groceries, tend the garden, and don't put these burdens on just one of you. This sign of respect and appreciation is the foundation for a loving and romantic bond.

- Enjoy a Do-Nothing Weekend – Just hangout with each other, no plans, be lazy, simply do nothing much, turn off computers and phones, let it unfold, simply be together. This can be very revitalizing and romantic, too.

- Volunteer as a Team – Easy, enjoyable and meaningful. Just contact your local food banks, Meals on Wheels, or other charitable organizations. Make a difference and do it together.

- Play Together – Have fun with cards, board games, and adding in some sexy "rules" can be very invigorating. Also, playing in the bedroom without cards or board games can be the best game ever! Endless possibilities.

- Dress and Groom Yourself for Romance – Make yourself look great, "clean-up real good," maybe a little sexy!

- Be Healthy Together – Get in good physical shape and stay that way by doing it together. You can help and be accountable to one another by working out together (stretching, exercising, walking, running, biking, taking a fitness class) and, as important, adopting a healthy eating lifestyle that suits both of you.

- More Physical touch - Increase holding hands together, more hugs and kisses, sitting close, snuggling, and gentle affectionate touching is loving, soothing, and can be the start of something more!

- Don't Go to Bed Mad – If there was a disagreement, makeup before you go to sleep. Communicate! Talk things out, be honest, share your feelings, be an intent listener, be sympathetic, understand the other's point of view, no carrying grudges, then

172

apologize sincerely, laugh together and hug tenderly. You'll both feel so good!

- Maintain a Great Sexual Connection – Do what works for both partners. Enjoy sexual intimacy ... whenever ... wherever ... and at any age!

Have Fun and Stay Young!

#93
THAI-STYLE FRIED RICE RECIPE

Here's a healthy and flavorful recipe that's fast and easy-to-make.

⇒ 2 cloves garlic minced

⇒ 1 onion chopped

⇒ 1 pkg frozen organic mixed vegetables, defrosted

⇒ 2 cup cooked brown rice

⇒ Sriracha sauce to taste

⇒ Soy sauce to taste

⇒ 1/2 c raw cashew nuts toasted

Sauté onions and garlic in a little water. Add mixed vegetables. When heated, add cooked rice.

Mix well and season to taste with sriracha sauce (spicy) and soy sauce. Top each serving with cashew nuts.

"Khaw ahroy!" – "Delicious rice!" in Thai

#94
INTUITION

Someone once said that intuition is knowing what we know without knowing how we know it! We just do!

Intuition is a deeply heartfelt "knowing" of something without any conscious reasoning. It is instinctive and not a carefully thought-out opinion or decision. It kicks in so fast that our minds can't keep up. We don't know or understand why we get this feeling, it just happens. It is spontaneous knowledge!

Intuition is often referred to as a "gut feeling." But we believe that it is a natural form of guidance that emanates from the heart, not so much the gut or the head. It is pure and untarnished from past experiences or external influences. It allows us to make decisions and assessments without even being able to explain or justify them. And these outcomes usually wind up being the wisest of choices.

We personally know from decades of experience that the best and most important decisions – big or small – we have made have come from our heart-centered intuitive feelings. We acted on just what felt good inside. This seemed to always work out well.

So, we advise you to be open to using your intuition. Heighten your awareness of these inner feelings and don't ignore them when you are faced with making choices.

Lead with your heart, more than your head. You'll be glad you did.

#95

DOES GETTING OLDER MEAN GETTING SICKER?

Why do most of us wait until we get sick before we try to improve our health? Wouldn't it be better if we tried to improve our health so we don't get sick? Just look around! More and more people in our community are overweight, sick, and have low energy. Heart disease is very prevalent. We all have family or friends with cancer or who died from it. Diabetes and obesity have reached epidemic levels. People are not living longer; they are dying longer!

The perception for many is that as we age, we expect to get sick. But we believe that it doesn't have to be this way. Getting older does not equate to failing health. We base our view on personal experiences of overcoming life-threatening illnesses, extensive ongoing research and years of healthy-lifestyle coaching on how to be young at any age.

Whether you are 28 or 82, the path to achieving and maintaining optimal health is to prevent disease and not wait until you get sick. It is our opinion and that of a growing number of acclaimed medical professionals that poor dietary habits, especially eating animals and dairy products, are a major cause of heart disease, cancer, diabetes, dementia, chronic pain, and other debilitating illnesses.

There is extraordinary power in food – it can be very healthful or very harmful. Preventing and even reversing illness is a direct result of what foods we choose to eat. If you eat well, you more likely will be well and if you don't eat well, your health is likely to suffer.

We encourage you to educate yourself on the foods you are eating now and also on the idea of a whole-food plant-based diet. Learn all you can about what foods are the major causes of failing health and disease. More important, learn which foods can prevent and even reverse disease. Hopefully, you will then commit to eating more healthfully. Consult with your doctor on this, but please don't fully count on his/her knowledge as most admittedly know very little about nutrition.

It's not as difficult as you may think. It's about replacing harmful eating habits with wholesome ones. It mainly involves eating less or completely eliminating meat and dairy products. Simply eat foods that are nutritious and delicious. Eat whole foods and not processed. Eat foods that are plant-based, not animal based. Eat more fresh vegetables including potatoes, fruit, whole grain bread and pasta, brown rice, beans, nuts, and seeds. And now you can choose from a wide variety of tasty plant-based meat and dairy substitutes at local stores. There is also an abundance of flavorful, high-protein, low-cost, and easy-to-make plant-based recipes on the internet.

It's your choice whether to gradually or fully transition to a plant-based diet by reducing meat and dairy consumption. Either way, you will be on the right path to improved health, vitality, and longevity.

We discovered long ago that eating a whole-food plant-based diet along with daily exercise did wonders for our health, energy and attitude. Pushing age 80, we both feel better than ever! It also feels good to know that we are supporting the welfare of animals, the environment, and our local farmers.

Getting older does not have to mean getting sicker. Changing the foods you choose to eat can add years to your life and life to your years. Why not get started now

Note: We are not licensed health professionals. The information and opinions we provide are based on our own personal experiences, practices and extensive research. Please get your doctor's approval before trying any new health regimen, including but not limited to diet and exercise. Ask your doc to join you! Have Fun and Be Young!

#96
TEACHERS

Most of us have had memorable teachers during our years in school. These selfless people not only taught us on the subject of our study but maybe passed on some memorable life lessons as well.

As life goes on, we learn from the everyday actions and words of family, friends, and strangers, as well. Also, most of us can be influenced by celebrities, politicians, world leaders, athletes and other well-known people. This influence can be helpful or harmful to ourselves and to others.

It seems natural for us to seek out and learn wholesome qualities from others that we admire and can replicate in some way. These can help us on our life's journey.

But wait ... there's more! We can also learn so much from those who act and speak in a harmful manner without considering the consequences. These are people who are unkind, selfish, bigoted, quick to judge others, bullies, liars and most often egocentric.

The idea is that we just observe their unwholesome and harmful behavior without getting into the drama ourselves. We stay calm and steady and allow them to become our teachers as well. They teach us powerful life lessons on how NOT to be!

So think about this next time you see someone who is behaving badly. Accept the reality of their actions and learn from them.

#97
TEN TERRIFIC TIPS TO CONTROL YOUR WEIGHT

As we get older, our metabolism slows down making it difficult to keep the extra pounds off. Here are some tips to consider for weight management:

1. Weigh yourself every morning before breakfast. People who do this are much more likely to maintain their weight than those who weigh themselves infrequently.

2. Eat until you are no longer hungry rather than full! You will actually eat 20% less this way.

3. Get some physical exercise every day. Whether it's walking, biking, gym workout, qigong, yoga, or gardening, be sure to get at least 20 minutes of movement daily.

4. Eat your main meal of the day at lunchtime and a more modest meal at dinner.

5. Take a short walk after dinner to help with digestion.

6. Don't rely solely on exercise to lose weight.

7. Cut out sugary desserts, snacks, and drinks.

8. Drink a glass of water before each meal, not with it.

9. Limit bread to one meal a day and make sure it is whole grain without harmful additives.

10. Cleanse one day per week - fresh fruit and a few raw nuts for breakfast, a fresh salad for lunch, and vegetable soup, salad, and baked potato for dinner, for example. No grains and, of course, no animal products or dairy.

#98
COMPLIMENT POWER

One of the most gratifying and spirit-raising techniques that we utilize daily is to pay a compliment to at least three different people. Yes, we make it a practice to say something nice or congratulate a fellow human being just to make them feel good!

It's wonderful to see a smile come to their faces whether they be friends or strangers. It's easy and fun and seems to spread exponentially. Paying compliments benefits you, the person receiving it, as well as the Universe.

It's an amazing little happiness tip! Why not give it a try!

#99
DUCKS and EAGLES

Decades ago we determined that there are two basic types of people ... the eagles and the ducks.

- Eagles would lead, ducks would follow.

- Eagles would soar in different directions, ducks would stay in their comfort zone.

- Eagles would buck the trend, the ducks would be the trend.

- Eagles would do exciting things, the ducks would settle for the status quo.

- Eagles would travel off the "beaten track," ducks would go to the same old places.

- Eagles would take action, ducks would quack and complain.

- Eagles would forgive, ducks would hold a grudge.

- Eagles would be accepting, ducks would be judging.

- Eagles would be open to new people, ideas and adventures, ducks are close-minded.

Being a duck or an eagle is a choice we make. We chose to be eagles. It's a lot more interesting and fun ... at any age.

#100
80%

Studies of areas around the world that have the largest number of centenarians (people over 100 years old) have this in common – people eat until they reach 80%! This simply means that they eat until they are no longer hungry rather than til they are full.

In contrast, American diets have been "super-sized" in recent years. Portions keep growing and so do our waistlines! Over 1/2 of the population is now obese in this country. The average dress size in the 1960's was size 8. It is now size 14! Unfortunately, all this extra weight has led to a huge increase in diabetes, heart conditions, and other health issues.

So try this eating tip that works great for us. Take a smaller portion of food for dinner. When you finish, instead of taking a second helping, wait 5 minutes. Although you initially felt like you needed to eat more, you will now feel satisfied. Make this a habit!

#101

LETTER TO OUR GRANDCHILDREN

Dear Jordan, Taylor, Ryan, and Joe ...

We would like to share with you some lessons that we have learned along the way in our life journeys. These ideas have enabled us to live extraordinarily happy, healthful, adventurous, and fulfilled lives.

HERE ARE OUR 25 "NUGGETS OF WISDOM" TO LIVE A HAPPY LIFE...

1. **Choose to Be Happy Now!** Understand that happiness is the journey, not the destination and not a goal.

2. **Express What You are Grateful For Upon Awakening Every Morning.**

3. **Look at Each Day as a Gift.** There are 86,400 seconds in a day – make the most of each one because you can't ever get them back.

4. **Go with the Flow!** Know that life's good times don't last and neither do the bad times.

5. **Practice Acceptance.** Process your life experiences as they <u>are</u> rather than how you <u>want</u> them to be. Acceptance over resistance is the key to inner peace and lower stress.

6. **Allow Space Between What You Experience and How You React To It.** Avoid quick knee-jerk reactions to daily situations, stay composed and only react after you've had time to think through your response.

7. **Make Lemonade from Lemons.** Continually put a positive spin on disappointments that may arise and make the best of everything that happens.

8. **Take Full Responsibility For Your Actions.** Don't rely on others and don't blame others. Think and do for yourself. Never feel sorry for yourself.

9. **Serve Others.** Make helping others a vital part of your life by volunteering and assisting those in need. Doing this takes the attention off yourself and does good for the less fortunate.

10. **Avoid Attachments of Any Kind.** Holding onto things and ideas can lead to discontentment and stress because nothing is permanent and things change. Learn to "let go!"

11. **Use Your Intuition as Your Guide.** Lead with your heart and not with your head.

12. **Continually Be Open to New People, Ideas, and Experiences.** Don't be afraid to take risks and make important life changes. Most often they will turn out well.

13. **Eliminate the Three Negative C's – Complaining, Criticizing and Cynicism!** These are unproductive and unhealthy habits. Catch yourself, then change yourself!

14. **Use Food as Your Medicine.** Eat mostly (preferably all) whole-grain plant-based foods to strengthen your body and build your immune system. At the same time, you will be protecting the Earth and the welfare of animals.

15. **Live Mindfully.** Be present in all you think and do. Avoid thoughts from the past or anticipating something in the future. This will eliminate anger, fear and worry and the stress that comes with it.

16. **Be an Eagle, Not a Duck!** Ducks follow the crowd, while eagles soar with independence, confidence and a sense of adventure.

17. **Abstain From Saying – "I'm too busy." or "I don't have time." or "I'm embarrassed."**

18. **Keep Stress Levels Low and Energy Levels High.** Take time to quiet your mind and increase your energy by practicing meditation, qigong, yoga, and/or other slow-down modalities every day.

19. **Be a Forgiving Person.** It benefits you as well as the person you are forgiving. Hold no grudges. Eliminate enemies by making them your friends.

20. **Remember that the Best Things in Life are Not Things.**

21. **Stay Away From Negative People and Situations.** Maintain a positive outlook for yourself and for humankind … and things will unfold in amazing ways!

22. **Spread Loving-Kindness.** Make the world a better place through <u>ongoing</u> selfless acts of kindness; being more thoughtful to family, friends, and strangers too; complimenting others; "paying it forward;" and just making people feel good.

23. **Keep Expectations Low. Judge Less. Love Unconditionally.**

24. **Have Fun and Enjoy Your Life!** Don't take things too seriously. Nothing in life is worth stressing over. Just say **"NBD" (No Big Deal)** and handle any situation by just doing your best.

25. **Live out Your Passions. Do What You Love and Love What You Do.**

May your years on this planet be as wonderful as ours have been and continue to be.

We love you all more than we can ever say,

Grandpa Bob and Grandma Fran

ABOUT US

During our lifetimes we have raised a wonderful family – three children and four grandchildren, enjoyed successful careers, traveled to more than 75 countries, became human rights activists, martial artists, mediators and negotiators, students and teachers in the Buddhist tradition, public speakers, international volunteers, and still serve as advisers to a number of non-profit organizations, businesses, and individuals globally.

We've experienced numerous exciting adventures, learned from many incredible wisdom teachers and we have overcome life's inevitable challenges including life-threatening illnesses. We are profoundly grateful to have been touched by countless wise and unforgettable people, near and far.

Long ago we made it our intention to stay young in mind, body, and spirit. Now, after many very happy and purposeful years, we are doing better than ever and feeling younger than ever... both pushing age 80! We are honored to share with others whatever knowledge and wisdom we have garnered.

We continually "live young" and lead happy, healthy, and meaningful lives.

Feel Good. Look Good. Do Good.

Bob & Fran

Disclaimer: We are not licensed health professionals. The information we provide is based on our own personal experiences, research, and practices. Please get your doctor's approval before trying any new health regimen, including but not limited to diet and exercise.

100% of proceeds from sales of this book go to counter the illegal trafficking of children and help empower areas of extreme poverty worldwide.

Bob and Fran's ACT Project ... to Abolish Child Trafficking

Website www.bobnfran.com

Made in the USA
Monee, IL
14 December 2020